Relax
and Come Alive

Other books by Iris Barrow

Your Marriage Can Work
Know Your Strengths and Be Confident
You Can Communicate
Fifteen Steps to Overcome Anxiety and Depression

for children, under the pen-name Bermingham

Hapi and the Morepork
Hapi and the Forbidden Island

Relax and Come Alive

Learn how to relax and manage stress in your life

Iris Barrow and Helen Place

Heinemann

HEINEMANN PUBLISHERS
Cnr College Road and Kilham Avenue, Auckland 9, New Zealand;
The Windmill Press, Kingswood, Tadworth, Surrey KT20 6TG,
England; 70 Court Street, Portsmouth, New Hampshire 03810,
U.S.A. Also at Edinburgh, Melbourne, Johannesburg, Ibadan,
Nairobi, Lusaka, New Delhi, Hong Kong, Singapore, Kuala
Lumpur, Kingston, Port of Spain.

This book is copyright. Except for the purpose of fair reviewing, no part of this publication may be reproduced or transmitted in any form or by any means, electronic or mechanic, including photocopying, recording, or any information storage and retrieval system, without permission in writing from the publisher. Infringers of copyright render themselves liable to prosecution.

ISBN 0 86863 444 1

©1981, 1986 Iris Barrow and Helen Place
First published 1981 by Motivation Inc. First published in this edition 1986

Printed in Hong Kong

RELAX AND COME ALIVE

Foreword		5
Chapter 1	Stress and strain.	7
Chapter 2	The importance of relaxation in our lives.	20
Chapter 3	Mastering the skill of relaxation.	29
Chapter 4	Breathe to come alive.	48
Chapter 5	Looking at your life style.	59
Chapter 6	Stress and your working life.	77
Chapter 7	Recognising reduced work fitness.	91
Chapter 8	Quality of life.	100
Chapter 9	Case studies.	106

*Last night
the crescent moon
hung sickle thin
low in the west.
The horizon hills stood starkly dark
whilst close to home
the plumes of the toetoe
feathered the last rays of daylight
and the black inked weeping willow
farewelled day into night.
The air was crisply fresh
with the feel of frost to follow.*

*The world stood still
in perfect peace
as day died
and the moon rose
newborn.*

*Alone in the twilight
the serenity of the scene
soothed my soul
and gave me faith
that there comes
each day, a new day,
each month, a new month,
to each of us new hope
and dreams anew
in the promise of the cycle of the moon.*

Helen Place 1979

FOREWORD

Today's fast pace of life takes its toll on people in many ways. The alarming increase of stress-related illnesses is perhaps the most obvious sign of how the pressure of living and coping in the twentieth century affects people.

As we advance in technological skills towards a more and more sophisticated way of life, the question arises, are we sacrificing our quality of life to achieve these advantages?

If we are losing much of what is worthwhile and good in terms of spiritual values, sound moral ethics, beauty of environment, a more relaxed and therefore better balanced life, then can it be said that we are really progressing? This question is being asked worldwide today.

Regardless of our feelings on these issues, we cannot halt directional changes or technological progress ... nor should we try to. What we can and should do is to preserve what is good, beautiful and meaningful to our way of life, while continually striving to improve quality of life.

Many things can improve the quality of life ... a purer and more aesthetically pleasing environment, better relationships, a striving for personal growth, better working conditions, and a more balanced lifestyle. In addition to these essentials, learning to function in a more relaxed way will result in better mental and physical health, important if a worthwhile quality of life is to be sustained.

Through learning to relax more on all levels we bring better balance into our lives, and therefore have a greater opportunity to achieve optimum health. In so doing we 'free ourselves' to cope better in every way. The long term effects become evident in the way we handle stress, think more logically and act more constructively, react to situations in a more positive way, become more tolerant in our attitude to and dealings with other people. ... The end result is usually a noticeable improvement in our coping skills, interpersonal relationships and sense of wellbeing generally.

In our work we see many and varied problems, the root causes of which can be as varied as the problems themselves. Nevertheless there are a few factors common to many cases. The state of tension in which many people continually function would be one.

Too many people are tense too much of the time; this adversely affects them in every area of their lives. It is no wonder they have difficulty in coping, and living happy and productive lives. It is almost impossible to assess and solve problems and take constructive courses of action to improve your situation if you are functioning in a state of continual tension.

Life is too short, relationships are too precious, opportunities too important not to be 'free enough within' not to grasp and enjoy these to the fullest.

We are *meant* to be happy, fulfilled through what we do, and moving in a positive way towards achieving a state of 'wholeness'. In experiencing a continual growth process on the spiritual, mental, emotional and physical levels we have the best opportunity of reaching this idea. Inadequate functioning through excess tension will work against our achieving this goal of total wholeness.

It is to *help* you achieve this, through learning to function in a more relaxed way in your *total* life, that we have written this book. Relaxation does not provide all the answers, but it does give some very important ones, and can act as a catalyst which will lead you to other answers. It will open doors for you. *Nobody* can function well unless they can learn to recognise and control tension ... this is what this book is all about.

In it we aim to teach you the basics of relaxation in a simple, easy to grasp way. We want also to emphasise the importance of achieving a good balance in your life.

Relaxation is a skill that can be learned in a relatively short space of time. With a little effort and consistency anybody can master it to the point where it proves effective in their daily lives.

We urge you to put in the time and effort necessary to do this. You owe it to yourself to do the best you can for yourself ... we believe that in learning to relax you will do this.

Iris Barrow & Helen Place

All names and case situations in this book are fictitious and do not relate to any specific living person.

Chapter 1

Stress and Strain

Although stress is an unavoidable part of living, the consequences depend upon your reaction of either *stimulation*, when you can see the possibilities within the problems, or *frustration*, when all you can see ahead are defeating difficulties.

What makes the difference? *Attitude*. And what shapes our attitudes? Our sense of being able to cope, of being in control, in contrast to the feeling of being pulled this way and that by people or events that we can't seem to do anything about.

Stress management is all about getting on top of the circumstance of our lives and staying there.

We'll begin by showing you just what stress is and how it happens. Stress can be very simply explained as resulting from a lack of fit between people and their environment, as this diagram shows.

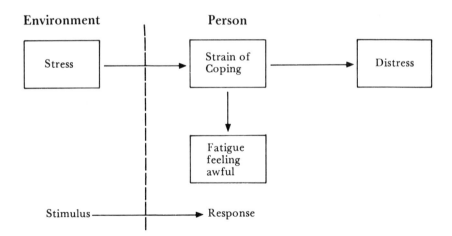

Stress can be easily imagined in the sequence of events that we only too often experience with a new pair of shoes.

Shoes are made to the standard pattern for the particular style, but feet have an individuality all of their own, unique to their owner. No two pairs of feet have exactly the same contours. Indeed, neither do the two feet of any one owner!

When we put this into our diagram we see that the environment — the *stimulus* — is our shoes, worn in all their newness.

The *response* is the rubbing on our heel, a cramped big toe, our pinched little toe, the *misfit* and discomfort that can lead to the *distress* of a blistered foot by the end of the day. After a time, we've worn our shoes in, they have stretched to the individuality of their owner and the stress is reduced and eventually disappears. We have altered our environment, and we are in control. Sometimes they never do become just right for us and when every wearing has a stress result, the shoes are in control. Eventually we cannot cope with the discomfort any longer and the shoes are discarded.

Life and stress have much the same sort of inter-relationship, except that with our shoes we know exactly what is the source of our distress.

It takes more time to isolate the stress causes in the many facets of our lives before we experience a similar stress relief. Fortunately, it is possible both to identify and to alleviate the adverse effects of stress in our lives by learning to apply relaxation and stress management techniques throughout the day despite whatever may be going on around us.

In the lack of fit between person and environment, there is a reaction that is both mental and physical, like this:-

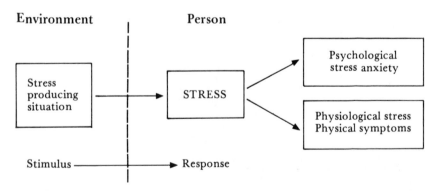

From the diagram you can see that stress causes fall into 2 categories — this is *physically* induced stress, from direct disturbance to the body by the immediate environment e.g. stress and fatigue from poor working conditions. Then there is *emotionally induced stress*.

This we bring upon ourselves, as it is the stress caused by a person's own thought. It is our reaction to our thoughts. So when we talk about teaching stress *management,* we're referring to showing you how to find out what's bothering you and then teaching you a response that reduces your feelings of anxiety and stress. Since each person has varying life and work situations, and somewhat different ways of reacting to their own situations, it is important that you take the time to really look at just what it is in your own life that is stressful. Usually, we feel that many demands are made on us, from our family, from our work and most of the time we cope pretty well, without any more strain than a good night's sleep will put right. But other times it all gets us down, and we feel that we just don't have the ability to cope with the pressures and demands upon us. That's when we feel anxious, depressed, nervy and upset. And that's when we need relaxation training to help us get over this down period.

In this book we'll take you through a programme to help you to use relaxation in those important situations in which you need it the most. You'll learn to notice when you first begin to experience stress and tension, and then to use these initial signs to signal you to use relaxation techniques.

You will also learn to identify tension-arousing situations and how to alter some of these problem situations so that your tension may not have a chance to get started in the first place.

Learning to do this will involve three steps:
1. We will get you to do some exercises to help you identify exactly how you experience anxiety.
2. We will help you to notice the ways in which stress is typically felt.
3. We will teach you the techniques of the progressive and mental relaxation procedures, the skill of momentary relaxation, as well as analysing your life style to identify and change stress situations.

By the end of this book, you will know how to use instant relaxation for stress reduction, and deep relaxation for refreshment and stress management.

Identifying Experiences of Anxiety

Anxiety is the common term we use to describe our states of heightened tension. Sometimes we may be tense because of specific circumstances, but at other times we may not really know the reason for our anxiety. (Such anxiety is sometimes called "free floating" because the experience of feeling aroused is not directly tied to particular situations.) It's important to note that anxiety is not something we "are" or "have". Rather, *anxiety refers to a group of specific reactions we experience in certain situations.*

Most of us notice anxiety in one of a combination of three ways. We experience anxiety *physiologically* (a racing heart felt in our chest, rapid breathing, or sweating palms). Anxiety is often felt *physically* (hands shaking, stuttering or twitching). Anxiety might also affect our thought patterns (thinking "I'm really getting up tight", of "Boy, an I blowing this one", or worse yet, "Wow. This will be a total disaster"). These thoughts interfere with the kind of clear thinking that would allow us to cope with whatever situations in which we find ourselves.

There are various methods you can use to find out how you respond when you're anxious. First, think back to the most recent time when you were really anxious. Try to imagine the scene as vividly as possible. Who was there? What did things look like? What was being said? Next, imagine that you are back in that situation now; try to include as many details as possible. Use all of your senses: sight, smell, hearing, touch and taste. What were you experiencing? Go over the details of the situation as they unfolded. As you *relive* the scene, observe your reactions. As you re-experience the stress and tension associated with that situation, identify your reactions. The checklist opposite will help you to pinpoint your stress patterns and tension reaction.

Remember that some stress is normal — it's impossible to live without some difficulties and frustrations and we sometimes need a fear reaction to escape danger. Indeed, for primitive man this was essential for survival. Benson, in calling this the "fight or flight response" in his book *The Relaxation Response,* explains that survival depended on the rapidity of using this response, one way or the other.

In the jungle of primeval living, if suddenly face to face with a predator, be it human foe or hungry lion, the human body swings into a series of responses designed to provide the extra strength needed to *fight*, and the stamina if *flight* as fast as possible was the wisest protective choice.

This reaction can be seen in the arched back, hair on end of a frightened cat, the enlarged pupils of a dog, or the speed of the gazelle running from danger.

Stress and Tension Responses

Physiological:

1. Increased heart rate _____

2. Increased breathing rate _____

3. Perspiration _____

4. Queasy stomach _____

5. _____ _____
         Other

6. _____ _____
         Other

Physical:

1. Shaking _____

2. Stuttering _____

3. Muscle twitch _____

4. Increased muscle tension _____

5. _____ _____
         Other

6. _____ _____

Patterns of Thought:

1. "I'm really getting upset" _____

2. "I'd better get out of here" _____

3. "I'm really making a mess of this" _____

4. _____ _____
         Other

5. _____ _____
         Other

In humans, there is an outpouring of adrenalin to ensure a maximum supply of oxygen and fuel to the brain, heart and working muscles by:

increased depth and rate of breathing,
releasing glycogen fuel from the liver store;
dilating blood vessels in brain, heart and muscles, and constricting blood vessels in areas not vital to immediate survival.

As a result the individual is primed for action — all systems are on *go*.

Civilised man still reacts to stress in this primitive way — and we need all these reactions in times of acute danger — but the fight or flight response is rarely appropriate in most of today's annoying situations.

Getting into a fight to solve a difference of opinion is right for your body priming, but is not socially advised. The result is physiological and psychological conflict with many uncomfortable symptoms — including high blood pressure, hardening of the arteries — leading ultimately to heart attacks and strokes. Fortunately, this *"alarm reaction"* can be changed to the *"relaxation response"* for lowered heart rate, metabolism and breathing rate. The point we want to emphasise here, is that it's not the infrequent dramatic events that are the only sources of trouble, but the many stresses of daily living that pile upon each other into a stress build up that put your body continually in a state of tension and "alarm reaction."

Thinking Stress

Underlying the physical and physiological reactions is usually an emotionally induced stress. With emotionally induced stress, the common feature is — *expectation* — the belief that something terrible is about to happen. Can you see the root of a lot of your anxiety in that?

The major personal problem for so many people is this anxiety. Or you may call it nerves, fear, stress or tension. And so often it is irrational fear. The purpose of stress reduction training is to teach you to get this anxiety under control, thereby reducing major stress related diseases and promoting a feeling of health and well being. Each of us brings to a situation our own particular history of involvements and reactions with various psychological stressors, and each of us has our own characteristic pattern of reaction and response. But it is not normal to be very anxious, to be feeling over fearful or always finding ourselves in high stress situations. Emotional stress has four general categories:

1. **Time stress:** This is an anxiety reaction to the abstract concept of time — that awful feeling that one "must" do something (or many things!) before some deadline; there's also a feeling that time is "running out" and that something terrible will happen.

2. **Anticipatory stress:** ... commonly called worry. Know what we mean? A feeling of dread about some horrible unnamed catastrophe. Or a feeling of anxiety about impending events. You can't name it — but it's a fear it will happen.

3. **Situational stress:** Anxiety from finding oneself in a threatening situation at least partically beyond one's control. This may involve injury or danger. More often it involves loss of status, significance or acceptance in the eyes of others.

4. **Encounter stress:** Anxiety about getting on with other people, about talking to them, meeting people. In a mild form this is shyness. In extreme anxiety at the thought of people contact this can be withdrawal from social contact.

Can you find the main cause of your anxiety in that list? We need to identify those situations, events, processes and possible happenings that we find most stressful to us, before we can begin to correct the tension.

The Tension Checklist

We'll start by collecting some base-line data on how tense you are each day and how frequently you experience tension-related symptoms. By keeping records each day for 1 week, you will be able to accomplish two important steps:

1. You will have a base level against which you can compare your progress as you learn to relax more.
2. You can identify particular situations and/or times of the day when you are most tense.

First, you need to establish a scale to measure how tense you are. We suggest that you use the scale on the Tension Checklist (overleaf). On this scale, a 10 equals the most tense or anxious you have been, and 0 equals the most relaxed you have ever been. For you 10 may be when you were being interviewed for your new job and 0 was how relaxed you felt after swimming while on holiday the previous summer. Or you may have felt that 10 happened a few years ago when your son failed to return home and you were afraid he had been injured or was lost; 0 was how you felt while lying in the sun reading a book. Write down at the top of the chart what 10 and 0 are for you, and then for practice rate how relaxed you are right now.

Each day you should write three scores on your chart:

1. Your average score for the day to indicate how relaxed you felt most of the day that day.
2. The score for when you felt the most tense during the day. Also, be sure to note the time, where you were, and a brief description of what you were doing.
3. The score for when you felt the most relaxed during the day. Again, be sure to record the time, location, and a brief description of what you were doing when you felt this relaxed.

In addition to recording these three scores each day, you should keep track of any specific tension-related symptoms you might have each time it occurs. (The chart lists some symbols you can use.) If you have a tension-related physical problem like headaches or stomach aches, it will also be helpful to note the time at which they occurred, where you were, and what you were doing.

Tension-Reducing Techniques

The skills to be mastered in this stress management programme are:

1. **Physical relaxation:** This involves learning the skill of deep relaxation, so that you can defuse the stress response deliberately, putting in its place the Relaxation Response. Deep relaxation requires a specific mental approach — you don't get it just by sitting or lying down quietly. It involves the opposite of the fight-or-flight response, for it is a passive attitude in which one "lets go" of tension, and is a deeply restful condition. People who enter this state for 20-30 minutes open their eyes later feeling a pronounced sense of peacefulness and release from former tension. Within a few minutes of returning to their activities they begin to feel buoyant, energetic and cheerful. These are feelings worth achieving aren't they?

TENSION CHECKLIST

Relaxation Rating: 0 = Most relaxed you have ever been
10 = Most tense you have ever been

Date _____ to _____

	Monday	Tuesday	Wednesday	Thursday	Friday	Saturday	Sunday
Average Score for the Day							
Least Relaxed Time							
Score							
When							
Where							
Situation							
Most Relaxed Time							
Score							
When							
Where							
Situation							
Occurence of Tension Symptoms							

H = Headache
SA = Stomach Ache
SP = Sleep Problem

Average score (add your scores and divide by 7)

2. **Self-management:** This is the day to day skill of learning awareness of your own internal arousal level, and of learning to respond to annoying situations with calm equanamity. This is when you learn to replace anger, anxiety and stress with the calm response of momentary relaxation, (you may prefer to call it instant relief!) Whereas deep relaxation is practised in private as a basic neurological skill for general well-being, momentary relaxation is a useful on the spot skill for dealing with situations that are likely to involve stress. This skill is a handy relief valve for pressure. Using it during your daily experiences will prevent the kind of chronic anxiety known as stress build-up.
3. **Life-style management:** This is the skill of continually assessing the relative balance of stresses and rewards in all areas of your life. This enables you to identify and then alter stress-producing situations to eventually avoid needless stress for a rewarding and enjoyable life style.

We'll begin by looking at just how stressful some life events can be.

The Holmes-Rahe Life Stress Inventory

The Holmes-Rahe list of stress-rated life changes has gained a great deal of attention as an assessment tool that seems to predict health breakdown as a consequence of stress overload. You may want to use it as part of your overall life style review. Doctors Thomas H. Holmes and Richard H. Rahe (1967) examined large numbers of medical case histories, looking for correlations between major health problems and the life experiences of the patients. They wanted to determine whether the relative amount of upheaval in a person's life — the extent to which his circumstances require him to change and adapt — could be used to predict the likelihood of serious illness.

The number assigned to each event is a statistical index of relative severity of that change for a large sample of people. Notice that some of the life changes listed are positive events (at least for most people). Nevertheless, Holmes and Rahe found that these events create upheaval in one's life with a consequent need to readjust. Take a few moments to go over the list and add up your own score. Include only those changes that have occurred in the previous year.

Holmes and Rahe contend that a person who scores below 150 points on this inventory has a chance of a serious health problem of less than one in three in the next two years. A score between 150 and 300 gives a likelihood of about 50%. A score of over 300, they believe, offers a risk of over 80% of a major health breakdown.

The notion of adaptive change as causing increased stress and general anxiety seems quite reasonable. Of course, the Holmes-Rahe inventory does not account for your own personal capability for meeting and dealing with stress, which is an all-important factor. For example, moving from one home to another may create tremendous turmoil and emotional upset for a family with already strained interpersonal relationships, but for a family whose members have learned to get along well and to take occasional upheavals in stride, the family setting may provide a sense of stability and emotional support to make the change less stressful.

The Holmes-Rahe Life Stress Inventory gives an index of the level of change and readjustment in one's life.

The Social Readjustment Rating Scale

Instructions: Check off each of these life events that has happened to you during the previous year.

Life Event	Mean Value
1. Death of spouse/partner	100
2. Divorce	73
3. Separation from spouse/partner	65
4. Detention in jail or other institution	63
5. Death of a close family member	63
6. Major personal injury or illness	53
7. Marriage	50
8. Being fired at work	47
9. Reconciliation with spouse/partner	45
10. Retirement from work	45
11. Major change in the health or behaviour of a family member	44
12. Pregnancy	40
13. Sexual difficulties	39
14. Gaining a new family member (e.g. through birth, adoption, older person moving in etc.)	39
15. Major business readjustment (e.g. merger, reorganisation, bankruptcy, etc.)	39
16. Major change in financial state (e.g. a lot worse off or a lot better off than usual)	38
17. Death of a close friend	37

18. Changing to a different line of work	36
19. Major change in the number of arguments with spouse (e.g. either a lot more or a lot less than usual regarding child-rearing, personal habits, etc.)	35
20. Taking on a mortgage greater than $10,000 (e.g. purchasing a home, business etc.)	31
21. Foreclosure on a mortgage or loan	30
22. Major change in responsibilities at work (e.g. promotion, demotion, lateral transfer)	29
23. Son or daughter leaving home (e.g. marriage, attending university)	29
24. In-law troubles	29
25. Outstanding personal achievement	28
26. Wife beginning or ceasing work outside the home	26
27. Beginning or ceasing formal schooling	26
28. Major change in living conditions (e.g. building a new home, remodelling, deterioration of home or neighbourhood)	25
29. Revision of personal habits (dress, manners, associations etc)	24
30. Troubles with the boss	23
31. Major change in working hours or conditions	20
32. Change in residence	20
33. Changing to a new school	20
34. Major change in usual type and/or amount of recreation	19
35. Major change in church activities (e.g. a lot more or a lot less than ususal)	19
36. Major change in social activities (e.g. clubs, dancing, movies)	18
37. Taking on a mortgage or loan less than $10,000 (e.g. purchasing a car, TV, freezer etc.)	17
38. Major change in sleeping habits (a lot more or a lot less sleep, or change in part of day when asleep)	16
39. Major change in number of family get-togethers (e.g. a lot more or a lot less than usual)	15
40. Major change in eating habits (a lot more or a lot less food intake, or very different meal hours or surroundings)	15
41. Vacation	13
42. Christmas	12
43. Minor violations of the law (e.g. traffic tickets)	11
Your TOTAL SCORE	

It's surprising isn't it, just how many things contribute to upset and stress, and how much change, even if in a positive direction, can be disturbing. This means that even with a lot of good things happening, like a holiday or a new house, there can still be stress reactions. This is where many people get confused, for they can't understand why they have felt out of sorts despite having everything the way they wanted it. That's why it is important to have the techniques, tools and concepts to minimise the stresses of living and working.

The goal is not to eliminate or avoid all stress. That's unrealistic — and dull, for it would mean eliminating excitement, a "fun" stress, and risk and challenege, an "achievement" stress. Instead, the aim is to keep stress at a level with which you can cope effectively whilst still enjoying the challenges of active living. You as an individual have the right to balance the total amount of life stress you experience against the rewards you get from engaging in the various activities that lead you to experience that stress. You owe it to yourself to design a life style that gives you the maximum of **personal well being.**

Chapter 2

The Importance of Relaxation in our Lives

In order to function well on all levels it is essential that we have adequate relaxation in our lives. Alas, most of us do not allow time for sufficient relaxation. Carrying this thought one step further . . . very few people know how to relax. We have had ample opportunity, through our work, of realising how few people really know how to relax, and if they do know, then how infrequently they take the opportunity to do so. Very rarely do people give themselves the opportunity to unwind on all levels.

To have adequate relaxation on our lives is one of the basic needs and we ignore it to our detriment. We have found that many people first need relaxation therapy (though initially be seeking help for other problems) before they can unwind enough to begin to deal with these problems effectively.

Far too many people are suffering from stress. Its effects are recognisable in the form of anxiety states, depression, psychosomatic illnesses etc. Too much stress prevents people from functioning as they should. Many doctors, recognising the effects that stress is having on a patient, will arrange for them to learn relaxation techniques.

The teaching of stress management and relaxation would be an important part of the work of many psychological clinics today. because stress is a problem that has assumed large proportions. It is also the underlying cause of many other 'presenting' problems, i.e. Joe Bloggs is sent along for help with his insomnia problem. It is discovered that the real problem is not an isolated one of insomnia (though of course he needs help with this too) but rather the underlying stress which is causing him to experience insomnia. What factors in his life are creating this amount of stress in the first place? Obviously the root cause of the problem must be sought. Regardless of the type of help that is needed, one thing is certain . . . Joe is going to have to learn the skill of relaxation and will have to learn to relax 'in a general sense'. He is probably going to have to look closely at his life and see if there is an imbalance that is adding to his problem . . . or even creating it.

In discussing relaxation we are going to talk about it on two dimensions which we will treat as separate issues. Firstly the art of relaxation itself . . . a skill which we learn as a specific exercise in order to relax on both the mental and physical level.

Secondly, general relaxation in our lives; in which we aim to achieve balance in the way we function, by allowing ourselves sufficient time to relax and unwind and by taking the necessary steps to do this. The second is essential to our wellbeing. And for most people, with the pressures created by the fast pace of life today, we believe the first is highly desirable.

Give Yourself Time Out

We all need to take time out in order to come to terms with ourselves and recharge our batteries. To get away by oneself to think, to dream and just to 'be', is important for many reasons, including the necessity of providing a healthy balance of relaxation in our lives.

It is very difficult to be creative, or even to produce on any worthwhile level, if we are not allowing ourselves the time and space we need to really 'be ourselves'. Only by allowing the necessary time to truly be ourselves can we get in touch with ourselves on a deeper level, and thereby work through to worthwhile conclusions. These conclusions can take many different forms.

Did you know that you are at your most creative when you are doing absolutely nothing? It's true. Many people believe that our greatest periods of recognisable creativity (and productivity on the deeper more withwhile level) are always preceded by a period of minimum activity. One of the laws of nature shows us this by the seed quietly germinating in the earth for what seems a long period of time with nothing to show. Then the plant emerges, grows and bears fruit. A period of intense activity preceded by a period of (seeming) inactivity.

Many artists have borne witness to this law . . . periods of inactivity in their lives have often preceded great bursts of creative energy in which they produced their most worthwhile work. There is an explanation for this. During this period of inactivity we give ourselves a chance to function on a deeper level of consciousness. Only when we mentally relax and free our minds from the necessary organising of thoughts and surface thinking to cope with daily demands, can things really begin to evolve from a deeper level within us.

We clutter our lives by indulging in so much hustle, bustle and frenzied activity that we lose sight of the things which really matter . . . and sometimes even the reality of life itself.

Our deeper thoughts, awareness, decisions about ourselves (and others) . . . the way we work through to a state of self knowledge and understanding . . . come to terms with ourselves and the issues that matter . . . all of these conclusions can only evolve slowly, by allowing ourselves the space and time to work through our thoughts and feelings regarding them. The force and depth of our creativity is dependent to a large extent on the opportunity we give ourselves to function on this deeper level of consciousness. Have *you* ever noticed a repeating pattern in your way of functioning, where periods of extraordinary creative energy   followed a period of notable inactivity, almost lethargy? We have. Here is a recent example of how this pattern operates.

Releasing the Creative Force Within Us

A few months ago we were consulted by a man who was in the copywriting business. His job was mainly creative in order to sell his clients' products. He came to the centre because he felt 'burnt out', and this frightened him. He felt he was losing his rouch. He explained that he had been doing what he termed 'hack work' for a long time now, and that his job depended on his producing vital and imaginative work. He was very low on creative energy at this stage, and had been writing all hours of the night trying to dream up inspired ideas. Coupled with this he was barely sleeping or taking time off to relax. He felt that with his low creative output he couldn't afford to.

It was explained to him that we cannot force either inspiration or creative energy, for they must naturally evolve from deep within us. There is no mystical 'tap' we can turn on at will.

Certainly we can take steps to try and trigger the release of creative energy, but if it is at a low ebb for one reason or another, then it is doubtful that it will flow forth in any noticeable way.

What we can do is create the right climate to encourage this flow. Our 'personal' energy level is one of the factors which governs the amount of creative energy we are likely to have at any given time. If we are physically exhausted or nervously drained we are unlikely to have a high level of creative energy. One artist friend told us that she can almost gauge her level of creative energy at any given time by the quality of her painting. She needs to be reasonably calm and peaceful to have a certain level of both mental and physical energy, before experiencing any noticeable flow of creative energy. Once more we come back to a basic law of nature . . . creative energy bubbles forth as a result of all else working in harmony.

Our client was told how this works for us as writers. When we are overtired or under stress the first thing affected is our ability to write. Even if we manage to snatch half an hour at the end of the day thinking "now I can get on with my writing", we'll still be staring at that blank sheet in the typewriter twenty minutes later, waiting for inspiration. Or if we do force ourselves along and get some thoughts down on paper we are rarely satisfied with it.

So through painful experience we have learned not to try to write when overtired or under a lot of pressure. We find it best to write when rested and relaxed, having achieved balance between work and play, activity and inactivity. We have also noticed that a period of high creative activity often follows a holiday.

As we discussed this more fully, our client began to get the picture and grasp the principle involved. We discussed his situation in depth, and as a result he decided to make certain amendments to his life. He immediately took a three week holiday and made it a time of complete mental relaxation. Afterwards he said he had spent a lot of the time lying on the beach and tramping through the surrounding bush. While away he also made the decision to balance out his life by allowing adequate time for relaxation.

In keeping with this decision he took up jogging when he returned home, so that there was a better balance between mental and physical activity in his life. He also allowed himself more time to potter around and be himself . . . and most important, he made a new rule that he would stop work at five-thirty and neither write nor consciously seek for inspiration after that time.

Another important move was to offload as much work as he could; he had previously been trying to cope with too much work himself, and consequently was firmly ensconsed on the work treadmill. He discussed 'pacing himself', by spreading his workload over a reasonable period of time instead of rushing at it and thereby exhausting himself within a comparatively short period of time. He also went into various other aspects of stress management, including the importance of giving total concentration to one job only at a time. This is sometimes called compartmentalising . . . and it works. The principle is to think of each job to be done as a separate small job in its own compartment and not see all the jobs collectively as one great huge workload.

In addition to learning other stress-management techniques, he began practising relaxation twice daily, and also started applying a one minute 'instant relaxation' technique six times a day. (Relaxation exercises will be dealt with in the next chapter.)

Within a two month period a change became evident; he started to develop a far more relaxed attitude. He decided that the world wasn't going to crash down around his ears if he didn't come up with inspired campaigns every week. We discussed this issue and he came to the conclusion that he had had enough experience in his work to coast for a while if necessary and still produce good work. Also that his fears about losing clients were a product of panic and were unfounded . . . in fact he ceased to worry.

As he mastered the skill of relaxation and began to enjoy it on a regular daily basis, his insomnia (a direct result of anxiety) disappeared completely. Soon he began to produce some really original ideas for his advertising campaigns. He told me he was 'getting back his touch' and that his ideas were the most imaginative he had come up with for a long time. In a nutshell, when he relaxed and let go things started to happen. From this we learn that if we give ourselves the chance to function on a deeper level of consciousness *we will do just that.*

We will come to know ourselves (and what is right for us) on a deeper level. We will work through to conclusions that matter, and we will give our creative energy the chance to flow. Eventually it will express itself in some worthwhile recognisable form . . . because we have set the right climate.

Most of us are so engrossed in the organising of our days that there is often little opportunity to function on this deeper level of consciousness. We are so bound up with the practical realities of just coping "I must do this — I must do that — I've got to get — I've got to be — at — by — I must remember" we have no time to sit and stare. Today's pace can and is damaging people.

We must take time to relax if we are to maintain our health and function on other than a surface level. We need to sit and watch the grass grow, and we need to do it often. It is not self indulgence or a waste of time to do this, for in doing so we are giving ourselves the opportunity to be more 'in touch' with ourselves and thereby meet the needs of the whole person. The busier the person, the more highly organised they have to be in their day to day living, the more they need to relax.

We will function better on all levels if we are wise enough to give outselves this essential time out . . . we will also reach a far deeper level of awareness.

Your Way of Unwinding

We all have different methods of unwinding. It doesn't much matter which method we choose as long as it has the desired effect, and as long as it does not demand the constant feeding in of surface and organised thoughts. Ideally, whatever way we choose to relax we should set the right climate so that our minds can 'free float' at least some of the time. Only by allowing this to happen can we tap our deeper levels of awareness and consciousness.

One person may arrive at this state through fishing, another through flower arranging, yet another through jogging or lying on the beach, or perhaps lying on the floor listening to classical music. The means by which we arrive at this desired state are unimportant. If it works use it.

Because we are individuals what works for one person is not necessarily going to work for another. We each have to find out what suits us best, and it is important that (A) we have something to turn to that has the effect of making us relax, and (B) that we use it frequently! Swimming and walking in a nature setting can be of great value; but it is equally important to simply sit in peaceful surroundings, doing nothing, and thinking of nothing.

To achieve that essential balance in our lives we need these frequent and regular relaxation periods. The busier you are, the more you need them. In addition to periods of relaxation, look for something which will absorb you to the extent that you will let go of organised thought and immediate concerns, that means something that has no stress factor attached to it and does not create its own tension.

You may say this is impractical for you because you're too busy. If this is so, we understand your problem. We too are very busy with work, writing commitments, homes to run and family interests to share, but we know from experience that if the measures to achieve a healthy balance in life are not taken, we will not function well. Sooner or later (probably sooner judging on past experience), the downward spiral begins when every aspect of life will be adversely affected. We function badly, running on reserve energy. When that is exhausted, what happens?

We have a limited amount of reserve energy; and we are extremely foolish if we continually dip into it. Unless we can recharge our batteries and build up our energy level, we will reach the point where there is nothing left. At this point the river has run dry and nature usually takes over one way or another, forcing us to stop and rebuild our energy level. Sometimes the method is painful, as in the case of illness or sudden collapse, but it can be a lesson that proves invaluable . . . if we learn from it.

The principle here is that there is a limit to our energy resources. *Reserve energy* should not be used unnecessarily, and certainly not over a long period of time. It is an extra to be called on in an unusual or emergency situation. We should replenish our normal energy as we use it through rest, relaxation, sleep etc. and always keep some in reserve. We will function best, by not draining ourselves beyond the safety level. Our work, self motivation, self esteem, health, relationships with others, enjoyment of life . . . everything will suffer if we are on a work treadmill or in a situation that demands too much of us. Imbalance is an indication of trouble ahead.

The Effects of Stress

It is commonly recognised that stress related disorders such as heart trouble, ulcers, insomnia, tension headaches, breakdowns etc. are reaching worrying proportions. Just treating the symptoms alone is not the answer. It is necessary to discover what created the problem and allowed it to go on developing. Sometimes a change in thinking and behaviour is necessary. Sooner or later we must face the reality of the situation and come to terms with what we are doing to ourselves.

Our responsibility to ourselves and how we can affect others by neglecting it, was demonstrated recently.

A man came along for help in dealing with chest pains for which there was no apparent physical cause. His doctor had given him a thorough physical examination and found nothing wrong, so had come to the conclusion that the chest pains must be psychosomatic in origin.

After hearing his lifestyle for the last twenty years it was surprising that he hadn't suffered a complete collapse. He had been trying to run three branches of a business for a number of years, and consequently had been completely caught up on a work treadmill, even working Sundays to cope.

Of course his family relationships had suffered. He never took time off simply to be with his family, and couldn't remember the last time he had been away on holiday with them. His wife was dissatisfied with their marriage and felt a poor second to his business interests. She couldn't convince him that it was *him* she wanted, his interest, time attention and not the substitutes his money could provide. She was a very depressed lady.

His teenage children had long since grown away from him and he felt he had no control or influence with them any longer. This worry was also adding to the general stress. He complained that there was no longer any communication within his family . . . but he didn't equate this to his not having the time or energy left to give to them.

As is so often the case he had tried to substitute material possessions for himself and his time. Communication started to improve within this family when he realised this. All of these pressures, overwork, unsatsifactory family relationships, had created stress which became too much for him to cope with. He had refused to acknowledge that this was happening . . . to do so would have demanded taking an honest look at his life and making certain changes . . . and this he didn't want to do. So he tried for some time to carry on as if the problems were non-existant and everything was alright.

However his subconscious knew that everything was not alright, and it told him so . . . hence the chest pains, which became so severe he could not ignore them. It was almost as if his 'inner self' said to him "I've been sending you signals for a long time now, but you won't listen to me. You've got to survive, so I'm going to *make* you take notice of what I'm trying to tell you.

This man admitted later that if it hadn't been for the severity of the chest pains which limited his capacity to work, he would have carried on in exactly the same way indefinitely. As it was, his condition forced him to take an honest look at his life, which resulted in his making major changes, albeit at first not very willingly.

After some weeks, during which time he learned the skill of relaxation, made the necessary essential adjustments to his lifestyle and tried to heal relationships with his family, his chest pains started to diminish in severity, and gradually ceased.

This man literally had to rethink his lifestyle and then follow through his conclusions by putting into effect new behaviours. This was not easy for him. He now has a much more balanced lifestyle, and reports that he is starting to enjoy life once more. His relationship with his family was the most difficult thing to alter. There was a lot of resentment there, which had built up over the years. However after a few very honest and painful talk-out sessions with them, the breach was gradually healed, though not without lots of ups and downs along the way.

This man was helped in time. Unfortunately there are many people who do not realise that there is imbalance in their lives, and that they and their family are suffering because of it. It is not until crisis point is reached that they stop, take stock, and begin to realise what has been happening in their lives.

If they are then prepared to make the necessary adjustments, and create a better lifestyle for themselves and their family through bringing better balance into their lives, the end result can be a much happier life for all concerned.

How is the Balance in Your Life?

1. Do you think you allow adequate time for relaxation in your life? Do you ever just sit and watch the grass grow? How long is it since you've given yourself the time to do this?
2. Are you doing anything that is creative and relaxing?
3. Do you ever get away by yourself in order to just be yourself?
4. Do you help those close to you to achieve adequate relaxation time in their lives?
5. What are you going to do now to ensure that you have this time in the future?
6. Do you realise the importance of giving yourself time for relaxation?
7. Do you love and value yourself enough to do this?

Where there is balance in our lives we are providing the right climate and the greatest opportunity for growth.

Without the chance to reflect and relax, consolidate and work through to conclusions about ourselves, little growth can take place. We need time and space to simply 'be'. As Socrates said, "The unreflected life isn't worth living".*

---

*Taken from John Powell's book *Why Am I Afraid to Tell You Who I Am.*

Chapter 3

Mastering the Skill of Relaxation

Relaxation as an exercise should be practised at least twice a day until it is mastered. It is like learning the piano; you are acquiring a new skill, and in order to master it you are going to have to practise daily. Once you are proficient at it you can then use it at will.

To begin we would recommend that you practise relaxation for about fifteen to twenty minutes at a time. Once, during the day when you are tired . . . perhaps when you first come home from work . . . and then again last thing at night just before going to sleep. However if these times don't suit, choose your own times; it is not important when you do it, only that you do it daily.

Once you have mastered this skill, you can use it when and as you need to. It's like carrying around your own special emergency anti-tension kit. If you feel yourself getting tense and uptight, you simply take a few moments out to apply your relaxation exercise. We have survived many a heavy day, when we have had to work excessively long hours, by taking a few moments out for relaxation.

Don't think of this skill as something that is only beneficial at the time you are actually doing your relaxation exercise. Its benefits should have a much more far reaching effect. You should benefit in every way and in every aspect of your life through learning the skill of relaxation. Think of it this way, we tend to function in either a tense or a relaxed way. You are aiming through your twice daily relaxation periods to *totally* function in a more relaxed way.

Through learning to control tension we indirectly lower the level of arousal in our central nervous system. With the many stresses we are subjected to in today's fast-paced way of life we are likely to quite frequently be in a state of heightened arousal within the nervous system; this is generally accompanied by an excessive level of muscle tension.

There are many sets of muscles in the body. If these are in a state of tension, they add to the general tension level in the mind as well as in the body. Here is a listing of the 15 major muscles in four groups. Note on this page, which muscles you find most tense.

Muscle group	Degree of tension 0 - 10	Is extra relaxation practise needed on this part?
1. Right hand and forearm		
Right biceps		
Left hand and forearm		
Left biceps		
2. Forehead		
Cheeks and nose		
Jaws		
Lips and tongue		
Neck and throat		
3. Chest		
Shoulders and upper back		
Stomach		
4. Thighs and buttocks		
Calves		
Feet		

If you have problems with any individual muscles, spend some time tensing and relaxing them, apart from your total relaxation practise.

There is a very close and sympathetic interaction between mind and body, so of course the state of one must affect the state of the other. Here is a simple example to clarify this. You are asked to speak at a conference and you are running late. Because of the stress this situation induces in your mind, it triggers off a certain response within the body and you become tense. There are a host of physical changes going on within you that are preparing you for emergency action. By practising relaxation you are going to save a lot of energy.

When we are in a state of tension the muscles act as partial blocks to the flow of blood through the body. As you know, oxygen is carried through the bloodstream to all parts of the body. If, because of tension this vital oxygen supply is reduced, certain things may happen. We may not have the same amount of energy and stamina, and consequently may feel more tired than we should. Mentally, we may even have memory lapses at times.

Once people have learned the skill of relaxation and are putting it into daily practise, they very often experience an increased feeling of wellbeing. They may feel more energetic or be more mentally alert. They may feel that they are coping better with everything. Naturally, if you are daily taking the means to break tension before it has a chance to build up to a high level, then you are going to experience the benefit of doing so.

One of the long term effects of functioning in a more relaxed way is that people tend to become more easy going, and because of this handle their relationships with other people in a better way. They often reach the stage where they find life more enjoyable. This is because they are developing a more relaxed attitude towards it.

The Opportunity to get 'In Touch' with Ourselves

Learning the skill of relaxation enables us to be far more 'in touch with ourselves'. So often we refuse to do this, either because we are frightened of becoming aware of what is really going on inside . . . or because we have so much pressure in our life we don't give ourselves the opportunity to do so. Whatever the reason, we are the losers.

Learning to relax lowers our guard, so that we can allow our true self to be known and felt. We tend to hold ourselves together so tightly, and to function within rigid framework and structures just so that we can cope. With some people its almost a case of "If I let myself go, even a little, I'll never cope, and I may not even be able to get myself back together again". So they continue to 'hold themselves tightly together' and force themselves on until eventually their inner self screams *"stop"* and will no longer allow them to continue. At this point the needs of the real person, which may have been suppressed and ignored for a very long time, begin to emerge . . . often very strongly.

We will function better in the long run by letting our guard down, thereby allowing our tightly-controlled inner self a chance to come through. Learning the skill of relaxation, and then adopting the principles of relaxation will afford the opportunity for these things to gradually come about.

Once relaxation is learned and applied it is possible for people to become very aware of themselves, perhaps for the first time in their lives. They become aware of the many physical sensations that are a part of their body. They may get in touch with their emotions, and become aware that there are certain feelings deep within that have a need to surface. Maybe these feelings have been supressed for years.

One man who had been unable to grieve for his mother's death, quite spontaneously began to cry and talk about her within a week of starting relaxation. Through relaxation we often become far more aware of the stirrings within us, and may well experience the desire to give expression to them.

Feelings that surface and are allowed to be expressed in a healthy way are safe. It is the feelings that are suppressed, especially over a long period of time that are unsafe. These build up in intensity and may eventually surface in unhealthy ways . . . or may be hard to handle when they finally do burst forth.

So if you experience a desire to cry when doing your relaxation, then cry. It is healthy and safe to do so. If you experience a desire to talk things out, then find a suitable person with whom you can do this. You may experience some unusual physical sensations when you are deeply relaxed, such as tingling in your arms or legs. Don't worry about them. Given the opportunity the mind has the wonderful ability to off-load its deep seated tension and frustrations through the emotions and the body. We have within us a special ability to balance-out and heal; we give ourselves the best opportunity for this process to take place through relaxation. By letting go and becoming more relaxed in the way we function, we are less likely to put up barriers that work against this natural balancing and healing process.

Should any feelings surface that you find hard to handle you can deal with them in one of two ways. Firstly by talking them out with somebody whom you trust, and who has the wisdom to in-depth listen to you. By doing this you are expressing and off-loading your feelings and dealing with them constructively. The second way is to write them out fully.

If you choose this method, keep writing until you are drained of emotion and everything is out. The act of writing out our feelings fully and holding nothing back, has great therapeutic value.

If you really wish to follow-through in dealing with your feelings, then write some constructive answers to yourself after you have fully expressed them through your writing. You can then destroy what you have written. The value lies in the act of writing out, not in keeping and re-reading what you have written.

From our experience we rate the first method as being of more value, if you do it with the right person because positive response and a little constructive feedback can greatly encourage you to open up still further. Some people however for various reasons don't find it easy to confide in another person, or can't find the right person. In this instance the writing-out method will prove a valuable outlet for them.

If you are still troubled by what surfaces once you have given yourself the opportunity to express it and deal with it constructively, then seek the help of somebody who is trained to help you in this area. A professional counsellor, therapist or psychologist is trained to help you accept, express, understand and come to terms with your feelings. There comes a time in most people's lives when the right help at the right time can be of real value.

What if you experience absolutely nothing during your relaxation periods, except to feel pleasantly relaxed. This is quite healthy and normal too. The premise is, that if anything needs to surface, then letting your guard down through relaxation will create the right climate in which this can happen . . . if it needs to happen.

Trust yourself and enjoy your relaxation periods. We have everything we need within to be 'whole' and healthy. All we have to do is provide the right climate and opportunity in which to allow these self-healing and balancing-out processes to take place. Let's look at a simple example of how this works.

When we become ill, in time we usually recover. Doesn't that say something about our self-healing ability? The bottle of medication helps, but without nature's healing force what could a bottle of medicine do? With a sprained ankle, we do nothing about it other than to rest it as much as possible, and maybe put a support bandage on it. Within a reasonable time it heals and is the same as it was before. What caused it to heal? The answer is the same. The more we function in a relaxed way, the more we give ourselves (nature) the opportunity to correct what needs to be corrected within us, whether it is of a mental or physical nature.

Once we are aware and 'in touch' with ourselves we become

increasingly sensitive to what is right for us . . . and what we need to do for ourselves in order to be healthy and inwardly content. The person who is 'in touch' in this way will know when they need to be alone, recharge their batteries, take exercise, talk things out, have more mental stimulation etc. They will be attuned to their body signals and will be in a state of heightened awareness concerning their inner needs. Sometimes they will even be aware that they need a certain type of food, such as eggs or fruit; given the opportunity the body will often let them know of specific needs.

The more we become aware of ourselves, the more we will develop heightened sensitivity and come to know our needs on all levels. In doing this we are opening the door to a deeper level of self knowledge and self understanding, enabling us to grow on many levels.

A Tense or Relaxed Body

Once the skill of relaxation is mastered we will be better able to tell whether or not we are functioning in a relaxed or tense state . . . because of our increased sensitivity, and awareness to ourselves. If we are tense our body will tell us, and we will be aware that we need to unwind and relax. If we are relaxed we will feel 'right'.

Often, until a person really masters the skill of relaxation they do not readily know what it feels like to be relaxed. They may have been in a state of tension for so long that it feels natural to them, and they don't realise that they could or should feel any differently. They may be tense when they sleep as well as tense during waking hours.

So many people who have recently learned the skill of relaxation have said "I thought it was normal to feel the way I did, but now that I feel so much more relaxed I realise how tense I was." Many people simply do not know how it feels to be really relaxed.

You will reach the stage when your body will let you know if you are tense and not relaxed. You will also become aware if any part of your body is tense . . . because it will feel different from the rest of your body. A tense shoulder will let us know that it is tense; it feels distinctly different from the rest of the body. When it is consciously relaxed the body feels 'in harmony' all over. When you become proficient at the art of relaxation, it will only take a couple of minutes concentration to deal with the tense member of your body and make it relax.

We can also lower the intensity of pain through practising relaxation. The pain of a headache can be reduced through practising relaxation, sometimes even to getting rid of it altogether. Along with lots of other people we have staved off impending headaches through relaxing in time.

One woman client had severe neuralgia pain, but because she was pregnant she did not want to take any pain relieving drugs. So she went to bed and practised her relaxation. Though it did not take the pain away, it did reduce it to a bearable level. She said afterwards she felt it had been reduced about forty percent.

Pain control through relaxation is not new. People have been aware of it and been practising it for a very long time now. This method has been used to reduce pain in childbirth and in other instances where pain control was needed. We tend to forget that we can help ourselves to an extent in controlling pain, simply by applying our relaxation skill. This is a bonus that goes with mastering the ability to relax. Relaxing may not eliminate pain, but often it can reduce it to a degree.

We cannot help but benefit from mastering the skill of relaxation, and it is worth while to put in the daily time and effort needed to do so.

Learning the Skill of Relaxation

There are various ways of learning the skill of relaxation, but I think that the easiest ways are either to take a course in it at one of the psychological or health clinics, or use taped instructions and master this skill through playing the tape daily in your own home.

Another way around the problem is simply to read a script on relaxation a sufficient number of times to become familiar with it, and then to try to apply daily what you have absorbed. We do not feel though that this is the best way of learning relaxation. Learning from a tape or being taught at a clinic would be more effective. A tape is a valuable teaching aid for you to learn the skill of relaxation through listening to it, but once learned, you take over for yourself and should no longer need to use it. It is always better to take over and do things for ourselves, once we have learned how.

Of course in times of extreme stress or when you are very tired or tense and have difficulty in letting go as quickly as you wish to, the tape can be a great help. It should be regarded as a back-up to the skill you have mastered, once you have learned relaxation . . .

but in the main you should be able to relax at will once you know how. You will benefit enormously from taking time out to apply your relaxation for ten to twenty minutes daily, for the rest of your life.

Regardless of the learning method chosen, you should practise relaxation twice daily until you master it. Once when you are feeling tired or tense during the day, and then again at night, preferably when you are in bed just prior to sleeping. By doing it last thing at night you help ensure that you have a better night's sleep. Sometimes the quality of our sleep is inferior. We may be tense when we go to sleep and not really relax when we are asleep. By practising relaxation last thing at night we help improve the quality of our sleep, and are more likely to awake refreshed in the morning.

Busy people may say "Fine, but I wouldn't have the time to also relax during the day." Our answer to this is "If you're that busy you can't afford *not* to". Even ten minutes of complete relaxation is going to help you feel and cope better.

Why not go somewhere quiet during your lunch hour and relax. What about when you first come home at night. There is great value in breaking the pattern between work and family life.

Some time ago the wife of a man, who had been counselled to do this when he first came home from work, said how much family relationships had improved. Previously he had been coming home tense and still mentally on the work treadmill, and trying to cope with the noise and demands of a young family. As a result he invariably ended up snapping and snarling at everybody, including her. Now he came home, said "Hi" to everyone, had a quick cup of coffee and went off to his room for fifteen minutes relaxation before getting involved with the family. To quote his wife "The difference in him is incredible". It seems that through doing this family relationships had improved considerably.

Most of us need a period of adjustment between business and family life. A period in which we can take off our work hat and put on our family hat. That fifteen minutes can make all the difference in the quality of the time we spend with our families. What if dinner is fifteen minutes later on the table. Does time rule us completely, or do we rule time insofar as we are able?

As mentioned earlier, leaning the skill of relaxation can be compared with learning to play the piano . . . if you wish to get results you are going to have to practise every day. It's the same with relaxation, through *daily* practise you will master it. There is no use doing it a couple of times a week and thinking you're going to learn how to really relax. To achieve worthwhile and noticeable results you should practise it twice daily. In an emergency situation, where a person is extremely tense or nevously drained, we would advise three or four times a day to begin with.

It is better to allow about twenty minutes initially until you are sure you have mastered this skill. Later on, once you can relax quickly, you can cut down to ten minutes if you prefer. It is possible to keep going for long periods of time, in an emergency situation where we may have to work twelve hours a day, through taking ten minutes out for relaxation two or three times during the day. However we wouldn't recommend anyone to work like that unless it is a real emergency. Such a work pattern would lead to an imbalance and consequently the risk of burning oneself out.

The time taken to master relaxation depends very much on the individual, the way they function, their habit patterns, their state of tension and general health. As a rule, we would say roughly three to five weeks, providing the person is consistently practising relaxation twice daily. That's not to say that they won't benefit in less time . . . many people feel better within a few days of starting relaxation. But to master it properly and derive maximum benefit could take that long. It would be unrealistic to expect a great change before then. Relaxation is another case where the rewards are worth the effort.

Overleaf we give you a practise chart so that you can fill in your daily relaxation times over a four week period. If you want to continue for longer than that, draw yourself a similar chart.

The Relaxation Technique

It is important to remember to let go with the mind as well as the body when practising relaxation. It is useless trying to relax physically and at the same time planning what you must do once you get up. We must work in harmony with ourselves, letting go on all levels.

Firstly, setting is important. Later on you'll be so skilled at relaxation you'll be able to relax when sitting talking to people if you wish. To begin, find a quiet pleasant spot where you won't be distracted. Be comfortable; recline in an easy chair with your feet

Relaxation Practise Sheet

	Monday	Tuesday	Wednesday	Thursday	Friday	Saturday	Sunday
Relaxation Practise							
When							
For how long							
Score before							
Score after							
Relaxation Practise							
When							
For how long							
Score before							
Score after							
Relaxation Practise							
When							
For how long							
Score before							
Score after							
Relaxation Practise							
When							
For how long							
Score before							
Score after							

Score Rating: from 0 — very relaxed to 10 — very tense.

up or lie on your bed. If there is anyone else about, ask them not to interrupt you during this time unless it is urgent.

Below we suggest several pleasant scenes for you to mentally concentrate on while you're relaxing. Choose the one that appeals to you the most. Mentally try to get into the scene. Or choose your own. You may well think of a better one. It doesn't matter, as long as it makes you relax mentally and helps you to block out conscious thought.

It's alright to let your mind 'free float' as long as it's a pleasant experience; but don't allow it to 'free float' on unpleasant things, or feed in the "I must do this, I must do that" type thoughts. If you start to think of unpleasant things or feed in active-type thoughts, concentrate once more on your chosen scene. This is the space in which your mind can 'retire' when you wish to relax.

Here are some suggested scenes; choose one or create your own —

Scene A: You are by a lake. It is a hot still day with fleecy clouds drifting across a deep blue sky. The lake is very still and glassy looking, it is deep green in colour, and round the edge there are ferns and foliage which are reflected in its clear surface. On the far side of the lake you can see swans drifting lazily along. Their grace and beauty are in harmony with the scene as they follow each other across the lake. It is still and peaceful and your eyelids grow heavy as you watch the scene.

Scene B: You are lying on the top of a high hill. You are in a sunlit clearing which is surrounded by bush and trees. It is a beautiful, isolated spot and you feel as if you could be on top of the world lying there listening to the call of the birds. Far below you can see the sea on two sides. It is very blue and it reaches into the distance. The long yellow grass you are lying on smells sweet and fresh and is soft to the touch. All the lazy sounds of summer drift your way, making you feel drowsy just listening to them.

Scene C: You are deep in a forest by a waterfall. Everything is very still and green; occasionally you see a native bird flitting through the ferns. You are lying on a bed of ferns by a waterfall which is cascading down from above and curling around the rocks in front of you. You hear no sound except the noise of the waterfall, and it lulls you as you listen to it. You can just see the sunlight filtering through the trees in places, but apart from this everything is intensely green. You feel as if you were back in the beginning of time, in a scene of unspoiled beauty and tranquility. It is unbelievably peaceful.

Scene D: (This scene will appeal to some people who hold the Christian belief.) You have come apart to the hills to be with Christ. You are very high up in the hills, resting with Him and far below you can see the plains, and on the distant horizon the outline of an ancient city.

You are leaning on a warm rock and He is sitting on a flat rock next to you, softly talking. The sun is setting, casting a golden glow over the hills as it sinks. You are remembering that he asked you to come apart and rest awhile in the hills with him . . . and you feel peaceful and glad that you have done so. As you talk together you realise His total acceptance of you, and this adds to your feeling of peace and 'rightness' about yourself. You become more and more relaxed as you share together; and watch the sun turn into a fiery ball as it sinks down over the hills.

Scene E: (This scene will appeal to people who prefer 'active type' scenes.) You are lying down on the bow of a yacht sunbathing while it skims across the water. The gentle rising and falling motion has a very soothing relaxing effect. A soft breeze sweeps over you keeping you cool and refreshed. A school of dolphins swims alongside and then drifts away. In the distance you can see land and it seems to change in colour and shape as you pass. It seems very far away, just as your cares and worries are far away and cannot reach you at this time. As the yacht continues to skim across the water its gentle motion lulls you into a state of complete relaxation.

Scene F: You are sitting on a hill above a paddock in which some horses are grazing. As you watch them the beauty and tranquility of the scene has the effect of making you feel at peace, and in harmony with your surroundings. The yellow grass on which you are sitting is ruffled by the wind. It contrasts with the lush green of the paddock below. There are three horses in one paddock, one white, two brown and a brown colt. The horses are quietly grazing, but every now and again the colt gets frisky and runs a short distance. Beyond the far hill you can see the mist gently rise and disappear. The scene is one of calmness and beauty and you feel totally at ease and in harmony with it.

An Exercise in Relaxation

Make yourself as comfortable as possible. Now slowly and deeply breathe in and out, gently pushing outward from the diaphragm as you breathe in, then exhaling deeply. Don't force or strain, just slow, gentle, easy breathing. Concentrate on your breathing for one minute. Gently in and out, slowly, gently in and out, in and out. Feel that your breathing is helping you to let go. As you breathe in feel that you are becoming more relaxed with every breathe you take. Release the tensions in your body with every breath you exhale.

Now stiffen the muscles in the calf of your leg. Feel the tension. Hold it stiff for a moment. Now let go. Experience the difference between the state of tension and the state of relaxation. Your leg feels quite different when you have let go doesn't it? This is how you should feel all over all the time . . . relaxed, not stiff and tense.

Now try stiffening your forearm, hold for a few seconds. Relax; once more notice the difference. Repeat; stiffen, hold, let go. Is any part of your body particularly tense? Neck, shoulders, chest etc? If you are aware of any part of your body being tense, repeat this exercise, concentrating on that particulat part. Repeat three times. Stiffen, hold, relax.

Now apply this exercise to the rest of your body from top to toe. Take it in sections if you find it easier. Tense, hold, then relax your feet, then your calf muscles, then knees, and so on up the body. Soon you will get to the stage when you will be able to apply this exercise simultaneously to the whole of your body. When you have relaxed the whole of your body in this way, once more go back to any part that is particularly tense (i.e. shoulder muscles) concentrate on relaxing them for a moment.

Relax physically, letting go as completely as possible, while you think about your chosen scene. Don't just see it, mentally get into it. Be there. Concentrate on it. Let you mind explore it fully. Experience the sensations of being there. Don't think about anything else right now. See and feel the colours and shapes in your scene, smell the air, feel the warmth or coolness of your situation. You are getting more and more into your scene. You are now giving your mind a rest and helping it let go and relax. Experience the peace and beauty of your scene. It is so peaceful, so tranquil; it's so good to be there, letting go. Just being there makes you feel calm and peaceful. Concentrate on it for a moment of two, letting everything else go; at the same time feel the whole of your body starting to relax more fully.

Feel the tension gradually leaving your body. There is nothing stiff or tense in the whole of your body. It is going quite limp and heavy, as if you were floppy and loose like a rag doll. Tension and stiffness have gone. You are letting go more and more with every breath you breathe in, just as your mind is letting go more and more as you rest in your tranquil scene.

Your whole body feels limp and loose and relaxed. A pleasantly heavy feeling comes over you as if you were sinking down, down, down through a feather mattress. Every part of your body is letting go and releasing tension, as though it is oozing out through your fingertips and leaving you. As this happens you sink into even deeper relaxation and feel totally at peace with yourself. Your whole body is now loose, limp and pleasantly relaxed. As if it had turned to fluid because you are not holding yourself tight or stiff any longer. You feel as free as a waterfall that ripples down and curls around the rocks at its base. Thoughts like free, loose, fluid and tranquil float through your mind.

As you let go and feel yourself sinking into a state of complete relaxation, you experience a sense of harmony within. Your mind and body are at peace and are working in perfect harmony for your greater wellbeing. You are at peace with yourself and a feeling of peace and tranquility wells up from deep within you. That is what you are going to experience every time you do your relaxation. And because of it you will feel better and cope better with what you have to do.

Let go, feel loose and limp, totally relaxed, at peace with yourself. The feelings of peace and wellbeing will stay with you afterwards, and you will cope in a more relaxed way. Now you feel deeply relaxed, and this will happen every time you do your relaxation. You will let go more quickly each time you do your relaxation exercise. Feel how good it is to be in a state of relaxation . . . your mind and body free from tension and cares. If you feel like having a sleep after your relaxation exercise, by all means do so, if time permits.

When you have finished relaxing you will feel alert, also calm, confident and at ease with yourself. All the tension will have left you and you will feel refreshed and invigorated . . . as if you have had a deep and satisfying sleep. The feelings of peace and wellbeing will stay with you.

Finish off your relaxation time with a good stretch and yawn.
Note: Don't be concerned if you don't experience all the things suggested to begin with, such as letting go completely, for as you

get used to relaxing and practising relaxation daily, these things should begin to happen. If they don't start in say a month of daily practise, you may need a little help in learning to let go. In this case go to a person qualified to teach relaxation and enlist their help.

Time Slot Relaxation

There is another exercise in relaxation which will complement your main one. It will also help you to prevent a build-up of tension during the day, and will have the effect of helping to keep it within controllable limits. For the sake of clarity we will call this *time-slot* relaxation. This is apt because it is done in two minute time slots. If you do this exercise at least six times during the day at regular intervals and also when you feel tension building up, you should be less tense at the end of the day.

One man, who was in a very demanding job told me that he used to leave his office at five thirty in such a state of tension he felt like a tightly coiled spring about to snap. Through doing his twice daily relaxation exercise, plus his time-slot exercise at least six times a day, he was able to control the build-up of tension. He did this so effectively that within one month of starting relaxation training he had reduced his level of tension to the extent that he felt only mildly tense by the end of the day.

Doing time-slot relaxation will help you relax more completely when doing your regular twice daily 'total' exercise. And the latter, consistently done will help you to more effectively apply time-slot relaxation. As we have said, one complements the other.

There is a great advantage in learning how to 'turn on' instant relaxation via the time-slot method. Supposing you are in a situation which makes you feel very tense, i.e. somebody verbally abusing you. Naturally you are still going to react to that situation, but by applying your instant relaxation (which you have trained yourself to do) you will become less tense and uptight. Consequently what is happening will not have quite the same effect on you. You will be able to 'bounce back' more quickly. If you do take action, you will do so in a calmer, more controlled way.

Here is another example of how 'instant' relaxation helped. Our client, who suffers from agoraphobia, stalled her car at a set of traffic lights in town. To make matters worse she was first in line on a steep hill. She felt panic rising. The she recalled her training, and immediately put into practise her time-slot relaxation, while still trying to get the car going. It worked; she felt panic subsiding, and as it did the car started. In a situation like this and the one previously described, it is a great help to know how to cope in a relaxed way.

The signal may simply be the word "relax", or it may be a body signal, such as hanging your hands when you are sitting down. Choose the signal that works best for you. It is possible to become so conditioned to relaxing on a certain signal that after a time you will do so without consciously thinking about it. One man told me that whenever he sits down and hangs his hands, he instinctively relaxes. Yet he is not consciously relaxing. He has now reached the stage where he is unaware that he is relaxing until he feels the lessening of tension.

After deciding which signal to use, simply try to *recapture the sensations of relaxation you experience when doing your regular twice daily 'total' relaxation exercise.* It's as simple as that. Firstly, try to remember your peaceful scene; give your mind a short rest by doing this. At the same time let go physically; feel your shoulders, arms and upper torso letting go and becoming looser, limper, heavier. Then feel this lassitude spreading all over your body. If it helps you to relax say to yourself words like – loose, heavy, limp, relaxed, tension going, fluid, easy, lassitude, tranquil etc. To start off with it may help you in recapturing the physical sensations of relaxation to say these words to yourself.

After a time when you have formed the habit pattern of regularly letting go, you won't need to say them. You will readily recapture the sensations of being completely relaxed as soon as you consciously 'let go'.

Two minutes at a time is all that is necessary for this particular exercise. It is most important that this two minutes be slotted into your day at regular intervals, and that you form the habit of regularly doing this.

During this time you are simply plugging into your 'relaxation memory banks' and recalling the mental and physical sensations of being completely relaxed . . . the same sensations you experience when doing your normal fifteen minute twice daily exercise. It's very simple, but like most simple things it is effective, and works when consistently used.

Some people become so adept at relaxing that they can do so when sitting holding a conversation with other people . . . and still actively participate in the conversation. While it would be difficult to get away mentally to their secret place, they could certainly let go physically and reduce tension in their body.

The benefits of doing both sets of exercise daily will be noticeable on all levels, and the long term effects will be incalculable. These benefits can only compound as time passes. It is something you must experience for yourself in order to fully realise and appreciate the effect it will have upon you . . . in every area of your life.

We hope by now you are starting to love and value yourself sufficiently to do something that is this important to your total wellbeing. Here are some ideas to show you how the stress content of certain areas can be reduced by the way you handle the situations. Remember that stress is a misfit between you and your environment, so that you find out what or where the misfit occurs and then deal with it. Apply relaxation techniques to alleviate the stress feelings, and correct the situation as we show you in these examples. As you can see, some of the correction involves ways of expressing your feelings and other practical measures you can take. Fill in your own pressure areas, and the solutions you will put into action.

Expressing Feelings of Stress and Tension

Situation	Possible Expression
Spouse tells you about children's bad behaviour.	"I really get upset when you talk to me about the children when I first get home. I realise you're upset. Can we set aside some time later tonight to discuss what we might do?"
Boss calls you in to examine your progress in recently assigned project.	"I have great difficulty responding to your request on such short notice and doing what I feel is a first-rate job. In the future, would it be possible for you to give me some advance warning?"

Your problem	Your solution
....	....
....	....
....	....
....	....
....	....
....	....
....	....
....	....
....	....

Changing the Environment

Situation	Possible Changes
Rushing from appointment to appointment.	Schedule appointments with brief breaks (e.g. 10 minutes) in between for relaxation.
Arriving at work feeling overwhelmed about tasks to be done.	Clear desk before leaving work on previous night; make list of tasks to be accomplished with time allotted to each.
Children's excitement when you arrive home in the evening.	Arrange for a 15-minute rest and relaxation period when you first arrive home.

Your problem	Your solution
....	....
....	....
....	....
....	....
....	....
....	....
....	....
....	....

Chapter 4

Breathe to Come Alive

Anxiety and tension in a person can be confirmed by their pattern of breathing as well as from tension seen so easily in the face — the strain and tightness around the eyes, the grimly set jaw, the hunched shoulders of muscles held in constant strain. Depression too shows, in the lack lustre eyes, the drooping, can't-be-bothered walk, and the overall air that the business of living is just too much effort.

So often we watch people come in looking so very tired and weary, hardly able to put one foot in front of the other, slumping into the nearest chair with a sigh of relief, as we wonder if all the skills of our training can possibly get them healed and on their way again.

But these are the easy ones to help, for they know they both look and feel at their lowest, and even if a friend, relative or doctor has made their appointment for them, they are ready for help. They know they can no longer cope on their own.

More difficult to reach are the ones who say there's nothing wrong with them and they can't understand why their doctor has recommended psychological help. Me, nervy? Why no, I've always been like this!

As we sit and talk, the breathing pattern gives its own message of anxiety, jumpiness, sadness or anger. Anger, when we're talking about tension? Oh, yes, indeed.

Some people are so angry about someone (more often *someone* than *something*) that they have to let all this out before we can begin to work through to a helpful solution.

For these people too, the breathing techniques defuse the current electric tension.

Breathing is the most basic function of your body. However, you probably take this important activity for granted without realizing the important part that breathing plays in your life, especially in your emotional responses. Breathing and emotional responses are closely related. If you have a shift from feeling reasonably calm and at ease to feeling tense, upset or miserable, your breathing pattern alters. Call to mind the short fast breaths when you're building up from annoyed to furious, and the die-away sighs of the apathetic can't be bothered state of mind. Of course, the opposite is also true. In relaxation techniques, the calming effect of deep breathing can be used to counterbalance emotional ups and downs.

Learning to relax and to breathe deeply will help to reduce stress and muscular tension at the thought of the things that make you anxious or at the thought of events or happenings you fear.

Much of our tension suffering is self-induced. We put ourselves into a shaking, twitching, unable to cope human being by letting our *thoughts* dwell on our fears. For so many people, these fears can't even be described or put into specific form. In contrast to the clients who come to us because of a specific fear (driving, flying, public speaking, crowds) or to those suffering in stressful situations (work pressure, relationship difficulties) many people seek help because they're overcome with fears of what might happen, if . . . And if . . . is anything and everything. As one client expressed it, she could be working away happily at her potting wheel, hands busy, mind free ranging, and suddenly the fears from nowhere came crowding in, like daytime nightmares. This . . . and this . . . and this . . . would all happen if she even so much as set foot outside her house.

This happens to so many, so that for them it is an ordeal to even get out to keep an appointment for help.

The trick in deflecting this smothering beneath the miasma of multitudinous and silly fears, is to stop those thoughts at the very first but what if . . . And this can be done by deliberately putting the body in a calm deep breathing pattern and letting the thoughts float right out of your mind.

If you tense and try deliberately to fight the fears in your mind, then they take hold even more strongly. It does require faith and belief in the relaxation techniques to "let go" at a time when strong attack appears the logical way to cope.

In the earlier practise sessions, the emphasis has been on learning how your muscles feel when tight and tense, and how to relax and free those muscles from tension. Now we'll go on to breathing and the letting go of your body into a relaxed state.

First of all, check how you usually breath by watching yourself in a mirror.

Notice first the *upward and outward* movement of the chest as you breathe in, then, as you breathe out, watch the *downward and inward* movement.

To find out whether your abdomen moves forward while you breathe in, turn somewhat sideways to the mirror. Put your left hand over the back of your waist and your right hand over the middle of your abdomen, so that your right fingertips just rest lightly on your left waist. Then breathe deeply.

If the space between your hands expands and your right hand moves forward with your abdomen, then you are using your diaphragm.

If you're not already doing so, then consciously practise this deep breathing. This diaphragmatic breathing is important for tension reduction, for with it you get a maximum amount of air with a minimum amount of effort, using both your chest and your abdomen.

For most people tension is not a lack of air intake, but rather a failure to allow the chest to relax enough so that the air can be completely expelled.

Breathing out should be a process of letting go. If you don't let go fully but still have some tension in your muscles, then some air stays in the lungs and subsequent air intake is restricted.

As you practise your breathing and relaxation exercises, let your chest muscles sag right down, so that all air is pushed out of your body. When you breathe in, start the breathing movement from your abdomen, pushing up as you breathe in. Establish a smooth, even pattern of breathing, concentrating on the "letting go" of each breath. It is the depth of that letting go that determines the extent of the benefits you feel from relaxation, for as you learn the art of letting go in breathing, your body will start letting go of old patterns of tension.

While you are relaxed and comfortable, your body free from tension as you begin to apply these techniques, you will become aware of the freedom from tension of your mind —

no anger, no stress,
no feelings of hopelessness,
no fears or worries.

This state of calm and ease of mind needs to be with us before we can begin to think positively about where we want to go, what we want to do, and to enjoy to the full who we are.

There is a very close relationship between physical body tension and the feeling of worry, fear and hopelessness; the feeling of not wanting to do anything, of being uninterested; the feeling of why bother, it's all too much for me, and the sensations of mental tension.

Our bodies feel tense and strained, and our minds feel that it is impossible to cope.

These feelings of mental strain and anxiety are too often attacked by pills and alcohol, instead of the acceptance of a very simple idea — that easing the tension of our bodies also eases the tension of our minds.

We can teach ourselves to be relaxed, to have a calm approach to life, and we can teach ourselves to get off a self-defeating track and on to peace of mind and positive thinking.

The beginning step is physical relaxation and freedom from tension. Since this process is aided by deep rhythmic breathing, here are some exercises to help you learn how.

Exercise 1: First of all, while you are lying on the floor or on a bed, feel the floor (or bed) push up against you, and the weight of your body pushing against the floor. Your knees should be up; feet flat on the floor. Notice what parts of your body touch the floor. Pay attention to any area that seems to be tense in your body. Tighten that area as much as you can and exgaggerate the tension. Now let it go completely. As you do that, breathe out. Tense as you breathe in, relax as you breathe out.

Now bring your attention to your face. Try to feel your facial expression. Pay attention to the tension in the many small muscles of your face. What is the feeling you are expressing with your face? Exaggerate that expression . . . tense it to the utmost. See what it is that your face is expressing. Give the expression a voice as if it could talk. Your face may say: "I am tense" or "This is silly," or "I'm worried" etc. There are an infinite number of expressions that come into your face. Let them come out of you if they want to — then let the expression go. As you do this, be sure to breathe out thoroughly four or five times. Then begin to breathe softly, being sure that the breathing out is not forced but just a letting go.

Exercise 2: Place one hand on your chest and one hand on your abdomen as you breathe. There should be a rise in the chest and the abdomen, then a collapse, a letting go, of the chest and the abdomen down again. Ideally the chest begins the wave, then the stomach rises; at the crest of the wave both chest and abdomen let go for exhalation; don't push, your natural body elasticity will force the air out. This movement should flow in a smooth wave so that it goes down your entire body, and with practice it will. Continue this breathing awareness until you feel completely relaxed and are breathing easily.

Exercise 3: Now take a deep breath and, *without* expelling the air, hold your breath and make the movements of breathing. Repeat this exercise four or five times, filling your lungs and making movements of the chest and abdomen. Stop and rest, and then do the sequence five more times. This exercise frees your diaphragm and starts the breath flow moving; it also gives you a feel for the exaggerated movements of breathing, and how close to this exaggeration you normally come.

Exercise 4: Begin to add some sound to your breathing. As you take a breath in, imagine the air is going completely down to the bottom of your pelvis . . . like a huge yawn, in which you fill your whole body with air. When it gets to the bottom let it go, *open your mouth*, letting the air come out of you very much like a sigh . . . a sound of release . . . (huhhh) a complete letting-out, letting-go sound. The vibration in the throat relaxes and releases that area. Continue to make the sound. It does not have to be a loud sound, but you should emit a sound each time you breathe *throughout the* *exercises.* Keep your mouth open. As children we used to make sounds all the time, but now as adults we are controlled and quiet.

Now you have begun to establish a diaphragmatic breathing rhythm, sounding as you exhale. The next exercises for freeing the neck and shoulders will help you to concentrate on a part of the body which frequently suffers because we hold ourselves stiffly or sit awkwardly at our desk, in the car or watching television. It's difficult to be a relaxed breather if the neck is tense. Each time you try to exercise a part of your body that is tense, your breathing rhythm may stop. If it does, go back, re-establish your breathing pattern and try to exercise the tense area again. You can — after

Breathing Exercises Practise Chart

Date .... to ....

Exercise	Monday	Tuesday	Wednesday	Thursday	Friday	Saturday	Sunday
Breathing pattern experience							
Chest — stomach breathing							
Freeing the diaphragm							
Letting go into sound							
Freeing chest and neck tension							

Which exercises did you find most beneficial? Why?
Which ones did you like doing the most? Why?
Which area do you need to concentrate on?

repeated attempts — break through the tension, freeing the area.

Work your way through each exercise in this manner, recording your reactions on the practise sheet. Let your breath pattern rather than the number of exercises be your guide line.

Note: It is especially important that you take care when practising your breathing exercises not to inadvertently move into a pattern of rapid shallow or unduly prolonged and infrequent breaths. Shallow breathing can wash out too much carbon dioxide from the air, and cause you to feel giddy.

Exercises for Relieving Neck and Shoulder Tension

Do these exercises six times each. You can do them night and morning or whenever you feel tension building up in the neck and shoulder areas.

1. Bend arms at the elbows. Rotate backwards in a circle. At the same time move shoulder and neck backward to coincide with the movement of the arms, then forward in the same way.
2. Turn head slowly to the left shoulder then slowly to the right shoulder. Repeat six times. Then move head slowly down to the chest and up back as far as it will comfortably go. Repeat six times.
3. Hang loose from the waist, bending forward, letting head, arms and upper trunk flop forward. Picture yourself as a rag doll swaying up and down and from side to side in a very loose relaxed way. Try this for a minute.

Movement and Tension

Movement is a natural part of being alive. If we are feeling at ease with ourselves and our surroundings, then we look alive and alert. The more alive and eager to enjoy life we are, the more naturally and spontaneously does our body move, and express our feelings We move gracefully.

If there is no movement, there is usually no feeling. If there is stiffness in movement, there is usually a restriction on feeling and experiencing emotions.

Death is *no* movement, *no* breathing, *no* feeling. To be wholly alive is to breathe deeply, feel deeply and move freely.

This sense of aliveness and inner joy is expressed in smoothly flowing movement that appears effortless. When you see someone moving slowly and expressing great effort through muscular tension, as though the journey were very difficult, you can feel their strain.

The person who is suffering tension and anxiety has none of this simple spontaneity, this sense of effortless movement and reaching out to enjoy life. Instead, there is fear in their faces, and awkwardness in their body movements.

Nowhere is the contrast between tension and confident joy in living experienced more deeply than in the sexual functioning of our bodies.

In making love there can be a smooth and flowing movement reaching a crescendo of excitement, then gradually decreasing to stillness and complete satisfaction. Or, there can be tension from the very beginning, not only by failing to breathe properly, but also with tense facial and body muscles. Simply put, any restriction of your breathing or your movements during lovemaking will rob you of sexual pleasure. It's a pity to have this happen. Unfortunately, we find this too often to be an underlying contributor of so many sexual problems. There's no doubt that tension and fear of failure can lead to just that, whether it be the spasms of vaginismus or the non-response of impotence.

Sexual response is controlled by our minds and our minds are the controlling factor in our body tension. So if we fear, we tense; if we are unconfident, we tense. And that tension has to be dealt with before beginning on the why of the fear. Often, this "letting go" into deep breathing leads to the unfreezing and freeing of long repressed incidents, that can then be talked out to give ease of mind. This is especially so for young people who find tension in those first relationships when they expected enjoyment; for people who are encountering sexual difficulties where previously there were none, in otherwise happy togetherness; and for others who find difficulty in making new moves when it seems as though every new approach ends in disappointment.

Angela and Bill, married and still in their teens, came in together to seek help for their gradually downward degree of sexual dissatisfaction. No, that really wasn't anything to do with technique, but far more to do with individual identity growth and trust within their relationship. Settling those issues was the key to renewed intimacy and enjoyment.

Cathy, in the depth of post-baby blues, couldn't bear her husband to touch her, despite their loving relationship. She learned the tie-up between strain and bodily responses, and he learned supportive patience. Since they didn't have a cassette player to listen to taped relaxation training, Bryan took Cathie through the various exercises, practising himself as well. Their care and concern for each other was a joy to know about, and both reported that the techniques did help to enhance response when their relationship returned some weeks later to the desired intimacy.

Gillian concentrated on the breathing exercises of relaxation for quite different reasons. After a bad attack of bronchitis some years previously, she'd always been rather frightened of breathing too deeply in case of pain. In the last year or so, she'd been to her doctor about asthma attacks. Since she had no previous history of asthma, and was going through the stress of city, job and house changes, she accepted that her shortness of breath was tension induced. That didn't make the panic feelings any easier to cope with when the attacks came. She still needed stress management skills so that she could begin on deep breathing as soon as the "attacks" started, preventing the build up of panic. As she became more and more proficient in the art of relaxation, her nervous attacks became less frequent.

Amy suffered from agoraphobia. For years she had been plagued with this problem. Whenever she saw a crowd, left the house, or was in the company of people she didn't know very well she would experience the unpleasant symptoms that are synonymous with agoraphobia. Sometimes her heart would pound and she would feel as if it was going to jump right out of her body. At other times she would feel such rising panic that she feared she would run away, screaming.

She was quite desperate when she finally came to the centre for help. As she put it, "It's getting so that I have to think twice about going to the postbox on the corner to post a letter." We reassured her that she could be helped but that nothing was going to happen in a hurry. Agoraphobia usually takes a long time to treat, though the person can feel considerably better within a short time of receiving help.

Amy was given counselling, relaxation therapy, desensitisation and 'reprogramming' therapy . . . in addition she was taught how to breathe to counter panic when she felt it arising. She was told to apply time-slot relaxation accompanied by deep rhythmic breathing every time she felt the familiar unpleasant symptoms starting, i.e. if she was in a supermaket and felt panic starting, instead of immediately rushing out and going home, she was to apply time-slot relaxation and deep rhythmic breathing on the spot. This would get her through the bad moment, and usually enable her to carry on. Once reassured that these bad moments would usually respond to this, and would *always pass* (usually within a very short space of time) Amy became confident about using her 'bag of tricks' as she called it.

It took time, but Amy steadily improved and was more and more able to get out and about. She says now that every time she feels an attach coming on she instinctively begins to breathe deeply and rhythmically; this immediately relaxes her, and very often the attack subsides before it really develops. Amy is now steadily progressing.

Deep rhythmic breathing has the effect of instantly calming us and bringing about a feeling of relaxation. It is invaluable for people who are prone to attacks of panic, for any reason, irrespective of its normal value in increasing our wellbeing and control.

Guy's job required that he frequently gave demonstrations and lectures concerning his work. Though very competent at his job, this part of it really worried him and he would find that he was suffering from extreme tension well in advance of having to give the next demonstration. By the time he stood up to give his lecture he would have constricted throat muscles and have a 'knot' in his stomach. His nervousness on these occasions was causing him real problems.

Guy was considering giving up his job because of these problems, but decided to try us first instead. We taught him relaxation therapy and the method of deep rhythmic breathing, in addition to discussing his feelings about speaking in front of others with him.

Guy began to experience less stress in his everyday life, as he mastered relaxation. He was advised to practise applying time-slot relaxation and deep breathing on every occasion he felt tension taking hold.

He got into the habit of applying it just prior to demonstrating or lecturing in connection with his job. By doing this he broke the tension cycle, and found that he felt a lot calmer when he actually began to speak. He was still a little nervous, as was to be expected, but it was a controllable nervousness. He found that by the time the instant calming effect of the deep rhythmic breathing was wearing off, he had become engrossed in his topic and was concentrating on it. He had always known that those first few moments were the worst for him, as indeed they are for many speakers. As he commented later, "Doing my deep breathing and applying time-slot relaxation, helps me 'slide into the talk' in a much less stressful way."

Now that Guy has proved for himself that these methods work, he is becoming much more confident about speaking before groups, and is no longer considering giving up his job.

Although, as we said earlier, breathing is so basic a part of our functioning that we take its happening for granted, these examples have demonstrated the benefits that can be experienced through using these methods of relaxed breathing.

Chapter 5

Looking at Your Life Style

Stressful Life Patterns

It's no good just learning to relax without also looking at your life style to identify your stress patterns. The skills of deep relaxation and self-management lead naturally to the assessment of one's total pattern of living and behaving. This involves the ability to identify sources of stress, so that you can remove or otherwise deal with them. For most people, this involves a reassessment of their general level of health and physical condition, as well as of the various facets of work and play which make up living.

Many people unknowingly subject themselves to unnecessary stress by adopting and maintaining patterns of behaviour, habits, relationships, activities and obligations that add to their stress scores day by day. During the business of living and working in our busy society, each of us accumulates a bank account of stress experiences, which in the aggregate help to determine our overall level of health and well-being. Too many stress points in too short a time, especially without relief and relaxation, will jeopardize our health.

A conscious review of your life pattern, from the point of view of stress accumulation, gives a clear and compelling picture of your stress patterns. The results of such a review, together with a new understanding of the physiology of stress and some techniques for stress reduction, can equip you to re-engineer your life style if necessary.

Type A Behaviour – The Heart Attack Pattern

Since about 1970, researchers in the field of cardiology have become increasingly aware of important connections between the occurrence of heart attacks and the life patterns of the patients. Heart attacks, and the family of related cardiovascular diseases, are beginning to take their places alongside ulcers as stress-linked diseases.

Medical experts have traditionally considered diet a primary causative factor in heart attack. This, plus possible hereditary factors, overweight, smoking, and lack of exercise, all seemed linked with heart disease. Recently, however, researchers have uncovered some important links between heart disease and a highly stressful life pattern that has certain distinctive features. Researchers still argue heatedly about which factors may be the first-order causes of heart disease, but evidence is steadily piling up to incriminate the high-stress life pattern as an important linking factor, or catalyst, in precipitating heart attack.

For a number of years, Friedman and Rosenman have studied the connections between heart attack and life style and have succeeded in describing a distinctive pattern that they believe represents the hallmark of the typical heart attack victim. In their book, *Type A Behaviour and Your Heart*, they give this definition "Type A Behaviour Pattern is an action-emotion complex that can be observed in any person who is *aggressively* involved in a *chronic, incessant* struggle to achieve more and more in less and less time, and if required to do so, against the opposing efforts of other things or other persons. Persons possessing this pattern also are quite prone to exhibit a free-floating but extraordinary well-rationalized hostility (p.84)". Friedman and Rosenman summarise the Type A pattern as one of chronic *time urgency, achievement, and competitiveness.* They believe the pattern comes into play only when the Type A person faces challenges from his surroundings. Apparently, the pattern is a manifestation of the way the individual sees his relationship to things and events in the environment.

Type A men were three times more likely to break down than Type B men were (Type B is the alternative to the intensive, overdriven Type A pattern). These findings led Friedman and Rosenman to study the Type A pattern in much greater depth and led them to the theory they propounded in their now famous book. We can consider the work done by them to offer very important and useful guidelines for personal stress reduction and stress management. By abandoning the distress-producing Type A pattern and by learning the more effective and rewarding pattern of achievement they call Type B, a person can re-organise their life and can gain protection from one of the most feared and most deadly diseases known to modern life.

Low Stress Life Patterns

Just as we find certain life styles to be difficult and stressful, we can also specify life styles that allow one to operate within an individual comfort zone of challenge and stimulation. We refer to the low-stress life style as one in which the individual consciously makes choices, undertakes experiences, and manages their own time and energies in such a way as *consciously* to minimize or reduce the levels of stress and the accumulated point count of stress experiences.

The first key principle of the low-stress life style is *balance* — the proper proportion of work and play, of challenge and ease, of stress and relaxation, of striving and taking it easy, of companionship and solitude, of exercise and rest, of discipline and self-indulgence. To achieve this proportion means arranging one's life in such a way that needs are being fulfilled in a balanced way, without an overload of any of the experiences or events that produce intolerable stress, and with enough significant challenge and stimulation.

The second key principle of the low-stress life style is *adaptation*, that is, the *psychological skill* of taking things in stride — of observing what is happening, of reacting strategically and maturely, and of letting provocations pass away and die out once they are over with. It includes the ability to relax physically and to unwind easily, the ability to monitor one's immediate reactions in stress situations and to consciously de-escalate one's internal arousal level at will. This is the basic skill imparted by stress reduction training.

A low-stress life style need not be boring or understimulating. Boredom and lack of challenge actually induce anxiety in and of themselves when they are prolonged and unrelieved. With a learned combination of adaptability and balance, one can continuously design and redesign a living pattern for the maximum in enjoyment, stimulation and achievement, with the minimum in unrelieved stress.

Notice that these descriptions of life style focus on behaviour — *what the individual does* — that contributes to the continuing stress or lack of it that is experienced. One's life style is a matter of choice, and although quite a few people would rather believe that their lives have been designed and programmed by outside forces, the key to adopting the low-stress life style is in accepting responsibility for the way in which one lives.

The Life Style Checklist, overleaf, contrasts some of the features of the antistress life style with those of the stressful lifestyle. You can add other items to this list, based on your own experiences and the way that you would like to live your ideal life . . . long, interesting and stress free, of course!

Life Style Stress Rating

Check the item which most closely applies to you.
I am most like . . . or this

Stressful Life Style Individual experiences chronic, unrelieved stress.			Low-Stress Life Style Individual accepts 'creative' stress of distinct periods of challenging activity.
Becomes trapped in one or more continuing stressful situations.			Has 'escape routes' allowing occasional detachment and relaxation.
Struggles with stressful interpersonal relationships (family, spouse, lover, boss, co-workers etc.)			Asserts own rights and needs; negotiates low-stress relationships of mutual respect; selects friends carefully and establishes relationships that are rewarding.
Engages in distasteful, dull, or otherwise unpleasant and unrewarding work.			Engages in challenging, satisfying, worthwhile work that offers intrinsic rewards for accomplishment.
Experiences continual time stress; too much to be done in available time.			Maintains a well-balanced and challenging workload; overloads and crises are balanced by 'breather' periods.
Worries about potentially unpleasant coming events.			Balances threatening events with worthwhile goals and positive events to look forward to.
Has poor health habits (e.g. over-eating, smoking, lack of exercise, poor level of physical fitness).			Maintains high level of physical fitness, eats well, uses alcohol and tobacco not at all or sparingly.
Life activities are 'lopsided' or unbalanced (e.g. preoccupied with one activity such as work, social activities, making money, solitude, or physical activities).			Life activities are balanced, individual invests energies in a variety of activities, which in the aggregate bring feelings of satisfaction (e.g. work, social activities, recreation, solitude, cultural pursuits, family and close relationships).

Finds if difficult to just 'have a good time', relax, and enjoy momentary activities.		Finds pleasure in simple activities without feeling a need to justify playful behaviour.
Experiences sexual activities as unpleasant, unrewarding, or socially 'programmed' (e.g. manipulating, 'one-upping').		Enjoys a full and exuberant sex life, with honest expression of sexual appetite.
Sees life as a serious, difficult situation; little sense of humour.		Enjoys life on the whole; can laugh at himself; has a well-developed and well-exercised sense of humour.
Conforms to imprisoning, punishing social roles.		Lives a relatively role-free life; is able to express natural needs, desires and feelings without apology.
Accepts high-pressure or stressful situations passively; suffers in silence.		Acts assertively to re-engineer pressure situations whenever possible; renegotiates impossible deadlines; avoids placing himself in unnecessary pressure situations, manages time effectively.
TYPE A		TYPE B

Balancing Your Interests
In looking at the various activities and areas that make up life style, we'll consider these general areas.

1. **Occupational/Professional**: Whatever you do that is your life's central activity; earning your living, homemaking, professional organisational membership.

2. **Financial**: Money, home, possessions that combine to give you security and shelter.

3. **Educational/Cultural**: The things you do for rewarding educational purposes, or cultural pleasure; reading, music, plays, art.

4. **Social**: Time, activities and relationships you share with others.

5. **Creative**: Activities or self-expression; hobbies, crafts, leisure pursuits.
6. **Personal**: Time especially for yourself and your own needs; solitude, spiritual, self-understanding.
7. **Sport and Physical**: Active participation in sporting activities; football, squash, swimming, tramping, walking.
8. This is an additional space to use to insert an area important to you not already named. Community, spiritual or political activities are some suggestions. Or it may be that you breed dogs, race horses or pigeons and that's important enough to be given a separate section.

To check if these aspects of your life are indeed in balance, look at the wheel diagram below, with these eight areas together forming the whole of the wheel.

You might need to put in some other areas of special interest to you for your long term use. But for now we'll look at these areas which form most people's lives.

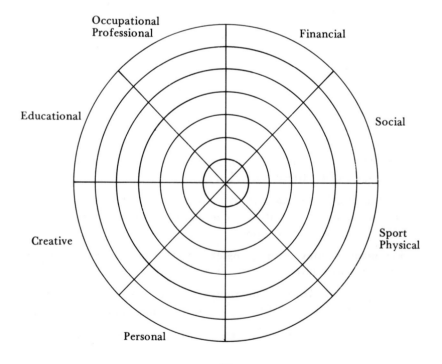

Now, think about each of the categories in turn for a while, and then make a general assessment of how much time each area involves. How do you feel at this moment about what's happening in that area of your life? What's the relative level of satisfaction with that area?

You will have noticed that there are graduating circles within the outer limits of your balancing wheel.

Start by considering the whole wheel as the total amount of your time and energy output. Now decide what proportion each area contributes to the total whole, and mark this on the nearest dividing ring.

Here's what Bill's wheel looked like when he'd finished.

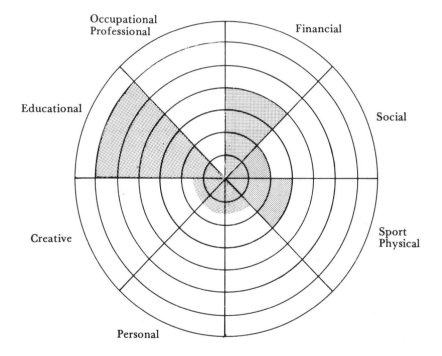

Bill works part time in a night job to support himself through university, plays squash once a week, and has neither the energy nor the money for anything much beyond that.

Bill resented the effort his life style took from his social life while appreciating the benefits of his long term goals. But going at that pace allowed no time for refreshment, and once the relaxation techniques were working well, we moved him on to the creative benefits of extending social activities. Bill liked to cook, but spent five nights a week in a hamburger bar and the other two nights eating barely interrupted study.

He began to have a few people in for dinner which he cooked (creative and social needs satisfied together), and much to his surprise, his term marks were better. A meal, and social contact made for a much more refreshed Bill who could then relaxedly still have study time before sleep.

What was yours like? Is the stress dissatisfaction you feel related to an area that's as little used as Bill's social, and creative life?

A definite dent in your wheel like that points to an area, or areas, in which you could benefit from trying some new activities, or perhaps drop some unrewarding ones from those areas which claim a large part of your time.

Time for Self

Here's another way to check out if a very common source of dissatisfaction applies to you. This is especially valuable for anyone suffering the poor-me blues, chronic fatigue and the beautiful home — beautiful baby — I've-got-everything — whatever's-the-matter with me feeling.

In this one, divide your circle into 4 areas, giving each area a size in proportion to the *time* each has:-

self; work; play; significant others.

Self includes time for your personal pursuits, interests, to be alone, to do whatever you want to do free of commitment and responsibility to anyone else.

Work is the way you spend the greater part of your day.

Significant others refers to other people whose needs, demands, requirements impinge on your life space.

Play is whatever you do for recreation.

Balanced they form a whole, as the diagram opposite shows.

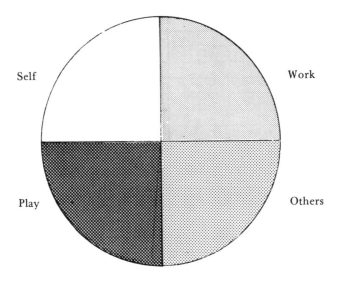

But quite often the full time homemaker finds her wheel is like this —

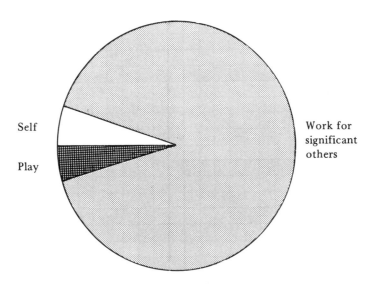

It is no wonder that she is perpetually tired and out of sorts — there's no refreshment for self in there.

The working mother, if she isn't careful has a life style like this —

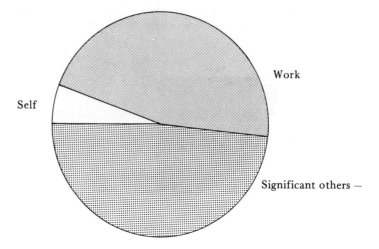

If her work is stimulating, then that frequently serves to counteract the mental blues of the previous example, but if its dull routine, then she has even less inspiration.

Sometimes both will have the additional stress from the non-support of an absentee husband, whose wheel goes like this —

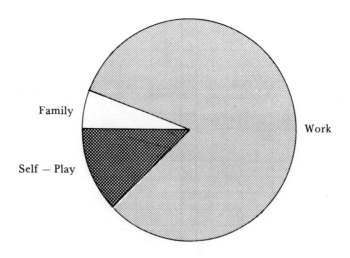

Work is Fun

Of course it is, and many of us steal that extra big chunk of work time from our personal and social selves because we've reaffirmed for ourselves that observation of Douglas McGregor,* that "work is as natural as play". But beware lest the stress pitfalls of the workaholic lead you to the ultimate in problems — burnout and loss of creativity.

Creativity is the vital spark that keeps us enjoying life and work, and it never flows from a tense and driven body. So take time out to play. Too often play is not refreshing, because instead of doing something we want to do, we go along with a significant other important to us, to please them. This means we feel resentful and tense inside, usually snap at the other person irrationally and ruin the leisure time for both people. Straight and honest communication about needs and preferences works wonders in stress relief. It is especially important for the work enthusiast to let work skills rest periodically and to use different skills at play.

What different skills do you need for balanced refreshment?

If you're people encrusted all day, will more people refresh or strain your evening?

If you work alone, is more solitude a treat or a torture?

Will playing bridge or a walk along the beach be best for you?

If you teach for your daily work, then will taking another class at evening school really refresh, even though teaching is just the job for you?

Would attending a class be a change or just too much of the same?

Or do you manage the switch off and over by moving from the computer world of your daytime to playing the drums in a dance band?

Have you ever given thought to trying something wildly different from anything you have ever done before — Eastern Religion at university extension, car maintenance at the technical institute, the local drama group for the lead in the next production, or Citizen's Band, scuba diving, or sky diving. There are just so many exciting options when it comes to replacing work skills with rest and recreation ideas.

In redesigning your life style, remember that a balance between all areas gives challenge, refreshment, time for self and others. If things are not balanced, what will you have to change? Decide what and where you will do more, and where you will do less.

*D. McGregor, *The Human Side of Enterprise*, McGraw Hill 1960.

Redesigning Your Life Style

Professional/Occupational

Do more of .... Do less of ....
....

Personal

Do more of .... Do less of ....
....

Financial

Do more of .... Do less of ....
....

Educational/Cultural

Do more of .... Do less of ....
....

Creative

Do more of .... Do less of ....
....

Sport/Physical

Do more of .... Do less of ....
....

Social

Do more of .... Do less of ....
....

Which area do you see as the top priority need for redesigning your life style?

Wellness Behaviour

It isn't much use aiming for a balanced and satisfying life style unless your body is in tip top working order. All of these aspects can be altered if you decide change is needed, but first you have to know what is your current level of well being. Be fair with yourself, but be honest.

The "Wellness Behaviour" Test*

This quiz will help you assess the behaviour patterns that establish your own wellness. Use your judgement to give yourself a grade — A, B, C, D or F, according to the following questions.

Relaxation

1. Do you take time to get completely away from work and other pressures, to unwind

Frequently	A
Fairly often	B
Sometimes	C
Seldom	D
I 'just can't'	F

2. Do you sleep well? Fall asleep easily? Sleep through the night?

Very well	A
Fairly well	B
Not so well	C
Have trouble	D
"Certified Insomniac"	F

3. Do you take, or feel you need tranquilisers, sleeping pills?

Seldom or never	A
Occasionally	B
Fairly often	C
Quite often	D
I'm hooked	F

4. Do you practise a form of deep relaxation (e.g. meditation, progressive relaxation) daily?

Nearly every day	A
Often	B
Occasionally	C
Seldom	D
What's deep relaxation?	F

Exercise

1. Can you walk briskly for a mile without becoming exhausted?

Easily	A
Fairly well	B
Can barely make it	C
Can't do it at all	D
Can't walk a mile	F

2. Can you play a fast game of tennis, or work strenuously for an hour without becoming exhausted?	Easily	A
	Fairly well	B
	Get very tired	C
	Get exhausted	D
	Wouldn't try it	F
3. Do you jog or engage in some other very active exercise several times a week?	Usually	A
	Fairly often	B
	Occasionally	C
	Seldom	D
	Allergic to exercise	F

Diet

1. Are you overweight? (Just check to see how much surface fat is visible on your body).	Not at all	A
	Mildly overweight	B
	Moderate amount of flab	C
	Well rounded	D
	Definitely too well covered	F
2. Do you smoke?	Never	A
	2 or 3 a day	B
	Half-pack a day	C
	Pack or more a day	D
	Chain smoker	F
3. Do you drink alcohol (including wine or beer)?	Rarely or never	A
	Socially & seldom	B
	One a day	C
	Several a day	D
	Can't do without it	F
	Average Grade	

*Adapted from *Stress and the Manager*, K. Albrecht. Prentice Hall 1979.

Lifestyle Redesigning for Stress Reduction

By now you are ready to put the various investigations together. Your "Wellness" average, your balance wheel, your life stress score (from Chapter 1) and the present state of your health will tell you most of what you need to know. In this assessment you have been estimating your potential for handling stress and the amount of stress you have developed in your overall patterns of living. Now we are focussing on the *personal* area of your balance wheel, for in here are the 3 factors, vital to health and wellbeing, in which are the key to your 'Wellness'.

These are relaxation, exercise and diet. So far we've concentrated on the techniques of relaxation, but this is not the whole answer for stress reduction and stress management in your life style. These three factors operate simultaneously to promote mental and physical wellbeing. Here's a brief outline of what is meant by each of these factors.

1. **Relaxation**: Any relaxation techniques you use to relieve the stress accummulated during your daily activities. This includes relaxation practise, (time-slot deep relaxation, meditation), refreshing activities − a quiet cup of tea after the family has departed from the early morning hassle, sitting quietly at your desk, letting your body unwind; a few minutes to yourself; relaxing music in the car.

2. **Diet**: A reasonably balanced combination of the basic nutritional needs of the body eaten in moderate quantities; minimal alcohol, no tobacco, no tranquilisers.

3. **Exercise**: Anything that you do − fast walking, jogging, squash, swimming − that arouses your whole body, uses your muscles vigorously, makes you breathe heavily more than 3-5 minutes and gets your heart pumping more rapidly and strongly.

By that definition, many people don't get *any* exercise. Golf doesn't come into this exercise category. Instead − place it under social recreation. How do you rate on those items? A relaxed healthy eater with a well established exercise pattern? You didn't make the grade? And you weren't even A1 on the Wellness test? Time to do the final correcting then. Here are some suggestions to help.

Relaxation

Keep up with your relaxation practise and keep the skill in first class working order.

Keep aware of your body and let go immediately of any tension that you feel taking hold, be it mental or physical.

Be a positive thinker at all times. Tension building negative thinking is a bad habit to be eliminated. Each day, give yourself a certain amount of time when you can be absolutely alone and uninterrupted.

Diet

If you're extremely overweight, get your doctor's advice and begin a weight loss programme. Read *Act Thin, Stay Thin* (Stuart R. 1978) to help you change your eating habits through behaviour change, or get psychological help. If you need diet planning help, get in touch with your nearest hospital dietitian or Weight Watchers Club. Form and keep sensible eating patterns. Many of the colourings and preservatives in junk foods are intensely irritating to the nervous system. Instead, have more fresh fruits and vegetables.

Exercise

If you are already into an exercise or sporting programme, keep the healthy pattern ongoing. If you're not, and never have been, have a thorough medical examination before beginning. A doctor specialising in sports medicine would be most helpful. Don't go to an overweight doctor, because that's a poor advertisement for health and fitness advice. Exercise is a long term investment and we're putting emphasis on healthy living, for what's the point of being beautifully relaxed if you're not going to be fit enough to enjoy to the maximum the benefits of stress management.

"But I hate sport." Many of us will still recall with horror the compulsory physical education of our schooldays, rejecting the New Zealand ethos of glory and fulfillment on the football field. This section is for those readers whose idea of relaxation is feet up, and a good book.

Warm weather jogging is too hot and sticky, cold weather running is wet and miserable, and in between times it's hardly worth starting a running programme is it?

Ugh, where's the relaxation in that? None for you, because well-being and health is as much in the mind as a physical state. You've always hated sport, don't want to rush out and join the nearest jogging club and are truly the product of this "era of physical passivity" as Kenneth Cooper describes it. (More of him later.)

The sport or exercise that is best for your fitness is *what you like to do*. If you force yourself into a training programme that you dislike, stress will increase. You'll put your exercise off — too cold, too wet, and suffer guilt pangs. You'll experience the dreaded sinking feeling as the set time comes closer. Obviously, mental health is declining and you've proved your point that sport is no joy.

Slowly and inevitably the forces of time make their point too. Perhaps you've always had an interest like gardening that's given you fresh air and exercise; been blessed with an equitable metabolic rate so that weight has been the same for 20 years, and switched off from stress with music and a good book. You are never sick, rarely have a cold and never succumb during the flu season. You feel healthy. You are relaxed, know how to control tension, and may not even look too closely your age.

But alas, this balance doesn't always persist. Later even if the weight stays much the same, it redistributes to settle in some mysterious fashion on paunches and haunches. Fair, fat and forty is the dangerous age, and now is the time to lay the foundations for a healthy eightieth birthday. You need to take especial care if you have a family history of later life weight gain, diabetes, coronary attacks and blood pressure problems, in your parents of grandparents. *Fitness after Forty* by Hal Higdon is an excellent book. *The Joy of Running* by Thaddeus Kostrubala, will have you believing in peak experiences, if not yet in the efficacy of exercise. *Aerobics* by Kenneth Cooper, and *Aerobics for Women* by Kenneth and his wife Mildred, is very useful. Aerobic exercise gets more oxygen into all parts of the body. Most of our daily activity exercises our muscles but it doen't do a thing for the heart and lungs, or circulatory system, and it's in this system that the stress diseases strike. Legs get tired in daily wear and tear, but they don't give up in cardiac arrest.

The aerobic approach demands oxygen and forces the body to supply it, resulting in a healthier heart, better functioning lungs and strengthened blood vessels throughout the body, so that toning up is from the inside out, involving all parts of the body.

That's the benefits to you physically. The benefit for you, sport hater, cold and wet and hot exercise hater, is that there's a wide selection of activities which can be used in an aerobic exercise programme. If you're not tempted by the swimming or the running, choose from the bicycling, (outside or stationary), walking, skipping, stair climbing, tennis, and even dancing to get sufficient exercise. Long enough to push your heart rate up to 130-150 beats a minute, depending on your age and the duration of the activity.

You can work out your own schedule, using the guides the Coopers give you, perhaps selecting a combination of outside bicycling when the weather tempts and indoor activities when it's cold and wet. Aerobic exercise can be enjoyable, even for the no-sport person. Dancing is a fantastic way to self-expressively meet the requirements. It is not too difficult to keep your heart beat up for five minutes to the accompaniment of *Zorba the Greek* or the disco rhythm, or whatever in fast paced style. And you can do it alone, whenever you want to and no interference from the weather.

For relaxed exercise there's nothing quite so peaceful as a brisk walk along the beach in the twilight of a summer evening. Before you know what's happening, you're going a little faster, alternating 30 seconds of walking with 30 seconds of jogging. A month or so at that gentle pace and you find yourself almost imperceptibly slipping into top gear, running not jogging. You — the sports hater — are enjoying it. Life will never be the same again. Running benefits every muscle group in the body, tones the arms, trims the stomach, requires little equipment, can be done at your pace, in your time, alone or with friends.

It's Up to You

Persisting in an overstressed life style is foolish. You have only yourself to blame if you are not enjoying your life; if you feel put upon by others with insufficient time for yourself; if you abuse your body with smoking, and reduce your wellbeing through neglecting relaxation and exercise.

See your life as a total entity, a grouping of many different activities and be sure that you don't become lopsided in any one area. Do not drift along in troublesome and stressful situations. Correct them before you spend weeks of time and energy in worry.

Be ready to explore new experiences, and set yourself a goal of trying something new each month, whether it be new places, a different restaurant, the activity you've always been meaning to try, a course at night school, joining the library, learning new skills, whatever takes your fancy. The list is endless as you open out to the self-renewing qualities of the life style balanced between work and play, self and others.

Chapter 6

Stress and Your Working Life

Stress, as the accompaniment of the rapidly accelerating changes of the 20th century, is so eroding the quality of working life that it must perforce become one of the major concerns of any organisation that wants to remain viable and alert in an ever more competitive world.

Where pressure is an integral part of the working situation, then it is vital that each person involved knows how to reduce the strain upon themselves, as well as how to manage their work situation for high performance but low stress. Is it possible to have a low stress, high satisfaction work life whilst also fulfilling the organisation's needs for productive economic performance? Certainly, if the basic rules are observed and the work situation is *planned* to be that way. Organisations require a person to work at an acceptable level of competence and capacity, whilst each person requires a task worth doing for adequate financial rewards, performed within a personally defined "comfort zone" of challenge and achievement. If that occurs, there is then a good fit between the person and their working environment. As we said in Chapter 1, stress is an outcome of misfit between us and our environment, and if we're uncomfortable, or operating outside of our "comfort zone" then we need to look closely to find out exactly what is the discomforting factor.

To define just what we mean by psychological well-being at work, lets look at how previous researchers in this field explain it.

At the beginning is the mental health of the individual and Jahoda writing in *Current Concepts of Mental Health*, (1958) stresses the importance of —

a positive attitude to self
growth development and self-actualisation
personality integration
autonomy
perception of reality
environmental mastery

The central theme of Konrnhauser's work, *Mental Health of the*

Industrial Worker, (1965) flows from Jahoda's concepts. Occupational mental well-being depends on the development and retention of goals that are neither too high nor too low for a realistic belief in oneself as a worthy effective human being, as a useful and respected member of society.

In *Work and the Nature of Men*, (1966) Herzberg associated the mental health of job satisfaction with —

knowing more
putting the knowledge to use
creativity
effectiveness in ambiguity
ability to be oneself
real personal growth — self as is, not a facade.

These are the essential psychological components which must be met if a job situation is to be satisfying. If such conditions are not met there will be dissatisfaction with the working situation and psychological ill-health, tension and stress arising from the disparity between the person's needs and the way such needs are satisfied.

Participants at N.Z.I.M. stress workshops have rated this disparity between "what I have to do on the job and what I would like to accomplish" as second only to the time pressures of heavy work loads in contributing to felt stress at work. It is possible that some of this disparity dissatisfaction may be because the person is in the wrong type of work for their personality, and ability, and to rectify this misfit requires self-awareness and often soul searching, if one is not to stay forever a round peg in a square hole.

More often the disparity is due to misalignment of personal and organisation goals. This satisfaction of personal needs and organisational needs is the prime management task for improving quality of working life. In this concept we're moving from the idea of work-health as accident-free and physical wellness only, to the idea of combined physical and mental wellbeing. Although work takes up such a large part of people's lives, occupational health has been a neglected field.

Cox tells us that stress at work may come from such areas as —

changes in work schedule
increased responsibility
decreased responsibility
change to a different line of work

trouble with superiors
trouble with colleagues
workload
boring, unchallenging work
role conflict
role ambiguity
(from *Stress*, 1978)

It is not surprising then, that for most people their work is at some time or another, a source of stress.

Role Related Stress

The concept of role refers to the expectations of the job we do, both in expectations of work output and the behaviours associated with the job. Think of it this way. The role of a professor or manager is vastly different from the role of the caretaker or cleaner of the building in which they both work, in terms of clothing, dress style, equipment, as well as in the work expected of each.

Our roles change many times during the day and we need flexibility to shift with situational change. Our parental roles are completely different from our professional working roles. Our role when seeking service outside of our own competency, is the reverse of the role we fill when working within the assurance and confidence of our own skilled specialty. Role related demands can be very stressful as one shifts between being a manager of . . . a subordinate to . . . a co-equal with . . . perhaps all in the space of five minutes.

Role *conflict* from the requirements of being all things to all people can lead to increased job tension and decreased job satisfaction. Sometimes the expectations associated with our roles are not clearly defined and this leads to the stress and strain of role *ambiguity*. Such uncertainty happens if we have inadequate information about job requirements and objectives, are unclear about the scope of work responsibilities and are not sure exactly what our colleagues expect of us. In other words we do not really know what's expected of us and why.

Do you do exactly what your job description says you do? Or have you found yourself hired for a position without even the formal outline of requirements of the job description, but been told that you'll easily pick it up as you go. The "pitching in" or "helping out" sort of job position many people find themselves accepted into, leads to a lot of tension for both parties.

Remember those NZIM results about stress from disparity? Does that happen to you?

Role related tension should be investigated whenever management is concerned about a low morale work climate. Studies have found that workers who suffered from role ambiguity and role conflict experienced —

lower job satisfaction
high job related tension
lower self confidence
greater futility
depressed mood
lowered self-esteem
life dissatisfaction
low motivation to work
Physiological stress of increased blood pressure
(Kahn et al 1964, French and Caplan 1970,
Margolis et al 1974)

Statistically these were not very strong findings, indicating that role ambiguity alone is not a major stress factor, but that it does have an impact on the total stress level experiences. Role ambiguity exists when a person has inadequate information about the work role, that is, a lack of clarity about work objectives. This means that the person doesn't fully understand exactly what is meant of them, or exactly what they're meant to do. This most often happens because job induction or briefing is not thorough, the person is left alone to pick up the system, or there are too many indirect or beneath the surface happenings — what is *said* to be done and not what is *actually* done.

Role conflict happens when a person in a particular work role is torn between conflicting job demands, between two (or more!) "bosses" who give directions, or having to do things which are not considered a part of the job specification. Role conflict is associated with poor interpersonal relationships, with inadequate information about work roles, and with responsibility for people and for things.

Both role conflict and ambiguity can be reduced by planning, and giving clear directives about desired results and responsibility for achievement.

Qualitative and Quantitative Stress

Qualitative — "too difficult" and quantitative — "too much" was a stress factor division made by French and Caplan in a study reported by Marrow in *The Failure of Success* (1973). They found that qualitative factors are not usually associated with occupational ill-health except for academic professors, whose publications must be first class if they're not to perish, and medical doctors, for whom the careless outcome is indeed the ultimate advertisement of ineptitude.

When we extend the definition of job difficulty to include quality of output, we find highlighted by counselling experience, two other groups for whom the quality of their work demands is highly stressful.

One is the new graduate in the first working situation. Equipped with the knowledge their degree implies, and eager to be at last contributing to the "real" world, their enthusiasm to make a valuable contribution is dimmed by gradual realisation that it's all more difficult than they thought it would be. This is really a transitional time of tension, of rapid acquisition of job-related skills (in contrast to job-related theory) as well as perceiving, decoding, accepting and using the values, habits, mores of the new situation. What seems to happen is that, instead of realising that this stressful state is usual in change, the person begins to feel inadequate in themselves and to doubt their own ability to cope.

If their lives contain a new marriage, or a new baby, a new home, or another city, and a new job, then you can see how the personal stress load is high in every aspect of living. There aren't many familiar wells from which to draw refreshing water for spiritual and physical replenishment. When even the sleep patterns are disturbed by restless reliving of the day's difficulties then a breakdown is likely unless the stress preventative measures are applied immediately.

Be aware that your new job can have underlying stresses, and be sure to schedule some time for your relaxation and recreation.

The second set of qualitative stress sufferers includes all those people who have to live with the public results of their decision making, especially when these results shape economic future or financial demise. Quite often, this stress is buried within the work overload quantitative factors, and we do not always acknowledge to ourselves just how deeply we can worry about the long term effects of the decisions made now.

The top executive team has the support of the group in reaching consensus as well as in implementing their plans so that any quantitative shock of non-achievement is shared. The self-employed entrepreneurs succeed or fail on the quality of their own ideas and efforts. Any person who wishes to practise their profession or use their skills in their own business must learn how to deflect stress and to take risks without losing sleep. Vitality and creativity are essential to the onward growth of the one person business, and you won't get this if your nights are spent in the restlessness of insomnia and your days in ulcer pains or indigestion pangs. Learn to relax and enjoy your work. Take heart that despite your hassles self-employment is a high satisfaction life style, if we are to take note of the work of Gail Sheehy reported in *Esquire* (October 1979).

Self-employment can also give one more control over the quantitative killers of overload, pressures and deadlines. Not always, for too often the tendency to do it all oneself begets an inability to delegate, the muddle on the desk takes so long to shift over in search of elusive documents and notes that organising and time management become skills one will learn someday — when there's time of course!

The pressures of deadlines are always with us, indeed, it would be a dull workload if there was no challenge of getting it done by or for a target reason. But you've only yourself to blame if you havn't learnt how to set priorities, plan time and work to that system. Oh yes, there will always be interruptions and the unexpected — build those into your organising. Never schedule a report completion for the day before it's wanted. Make the target date a 2-3 days, even a week, beforehand. That gives the time to cope with the otherwise panic of the unexpected, as well as giving you the sense of being in control of your environment. That's more job satisfaction and less need to treat your stress suffering in non-productive ways.

The clear desk perfection pattern is a common self-induced stress source. It usually starts as a self-set standard of performance, when the demands of the job are not unduly great and can be easily contained in the amount of effort required to deal with the paper work before the end of each day. A clear desk, and a sense of accomplishment gives a clear mind to relax and enjoy the evening without worries. But what if the job changes, or a new job situation brings an altogether different set of demands so that the past pattern of clearing the desk each day is just no longer physically possible.

Nor is it needed, for not all that paper is required filed as *finished today*.

Persons caught in this trap suffer agonies in tension as they feel their abilities and standards are slipping. No longer good performers according to their previous standards, they begin to feel failure and before long, their stress suffering does impair their achievement. Many highly perfectionistic-every-detail-attended-to-personally people sink beneath this load, or muddle through it aided by tranquilisers. The medication does ease the suffering and help you to cope, in the short term, but it must be accompanied by a long term plan of acquiring relaxation skills, and learning how to sort priorities for the day's events, and walking away from work on your desk that you've decided is tomorrow's task.

Studies have shown that as well as overall work dissatisfaction, the overload factors were significantly related to escapist drinking, absenteeism, lowered self-esteem, and a lowered interest and motivation to work.

The Job-person Fit

These stress indicators can be summarised into three groups.

1. **Factors within the person.** Each person brings their own unique combination of skills, characteristics, personality with them into the situation.

2. **Factors within the job.** These are the potential sources of stress in the work environment itself.

3. **Factors external to person and work life.** These are the extra-organisational variables such as family problems, financial problems etc., which means that the person comes to work affected by whatever is happening to them in their life outside of work.

The central feature of stress at work is that every person with their own personality, their own individual skills and abilities, and their own set of outside influences, must come along each day and fit into a specific work situation. All may flow together in a satisfying and productive day, or any one of the factors may be out of kilter to produce "one of *those* days".

At one time or another, everyone of us has had such a day. The neighbours had a noisy party, we didn't sleep well, got up late, missed the bus and arrived too late to review reports before an important meeting. You know the feelings of tension from every source.

We refer to this as the person-job fit, and you can see how these three areas combine in this model.

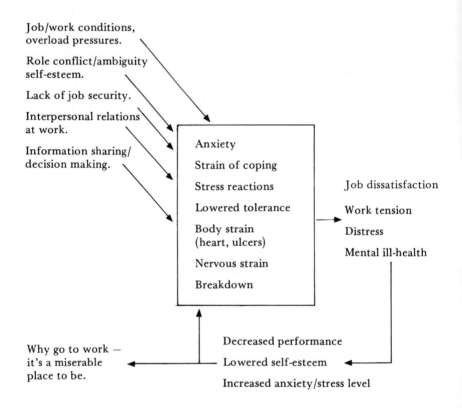

To find why there is stress in situations we're using the concept of stress as a lack of fit between people and their work environment, with stress being an individual perceptual response rooted in psychological processes.

So we start with the person in the work situation and then move onto the consequences of that person not fitting into the situation, or of the situation not being able to give and take, not being flexible enough to adapt to the people who come into it. Either way, the stress response for the person is shown in the diagram opposite.

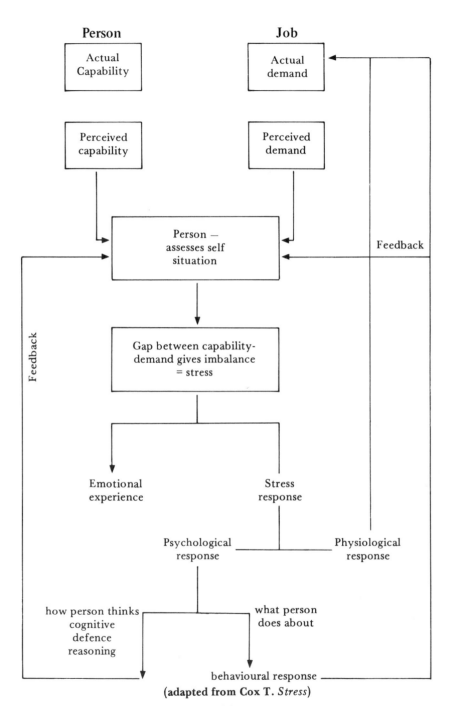
(adapted from Cox T. *Stress*)

This diagram of how the person-fit system produces stress has five stages.

1. The actual demands of the situation, and the actual capabilities of the person.
2. The person's perception of the demand and perception of ability to cope with it.
3. If there is a gap between what the person sees as required and their possessed abilities/skills to meet the demand, then stress is experienced.
   There are emotional feelings of stress, physiological changes and cognitive and behavioural attempts to cope with the stress demands.
4. From this, the person moves into the stage of living with the consequences of the coping responses selected and used.
5. The final stage is of feedback, in which the person assesses the effectiveness of the stress response in coping.

Stress in this transactional model is thus seen as developing from a particular sort of relationship between the person and environment. Stress arises from a person's comparison between the demand on them and their ability to cope. An imbalance in this mechanism, when coping is important, gives rise to the experience of stress and to stress response, as a means of coping with the source of stress.

Stress Symptoms

The psychological aspects of coping involve both mental cognitive and behavioural strategies and when it comes to uncovering cause and effect or assessing stress sources in a work situation, some areas to be looked at include:-

   absences due to illness
   accidents
   repeated work, mistakes
   work methods
   working conditions
   job responsibility
   personal autonomy
   fatigue, boredom

work peaks, overload
job satisfaction — need met or not
job content — variation, challenge
supervision, leadership
interpersonal relationships
work climate

That by no means exhausted list makes for a lot of variables which can be looked at.

Counselling the Work Stressed

People overburdened and uncomfortable from stress symptoms consult their doctor when they can no longer cope on their own. For them, medicare for their dyspepsia and headaches, or pills for sleeping are but a temporary alleviative measure and they're referred to us for indepth help.

It's our job to probe out the misfit of person and their environment and our findings are almost always that the symptoms are related to specific sets of happenings in their working life. These sets can be broadly clustered into three areas:-

1. People responsibility; 2. Wrong job; 3. Work overload.

Andrew, aged twenty one, had gone to his doctor for stomach pain relief and was somewhat disbelieving that it could be tension related. After all he'd passed his exams with no problem, enjoyed his sport and social life, lived peacefully at home, so really, how could it all be stress, especially when his job was progressing well too. What could it possibly have to do with work? Plenty, as it turned out.

Andrew looked alert and lively. He had been with the same company since leaving school and gained technical qualifications while he worked. All in all, a responsible, intelligent, likeable young man. So why should life, so comfortable previously, now suddenly have soured. He felt that there really must be a physical cause for his pain, only something like a tumour could make him feel so awful.

We began to explore exactly what had been happening in his environment when he became aware of the pain of stress symptoms. A few months previously he'd been promoted into his first supervisory position, the usual progression after passing his exams in science and laboratory work. For the first time he had to get results through others. He'd started on the management path of being responsible for people and their output, and he didn't know how. There was no previous experience in his work to prepare him, and no training in people skills was given by his company to help him.

This is a common cause of work stress and one that could so easily be avoided, if management did it's job properly and prepared people adequately for their next moves within a clearly defined career management plan.

For their immediate relief, people like Andrew can learn the stress management techniques to enable them to cope. But continued long term ease requires attending to the job-person misfit. In this case Andrew needed counselling support to give him the confidence to speak up and ask to go on an appropriate training course, since the business didn't run in-company training courses. Two years later, Andrew reported that he was well into studying for an NZIM management diploma and had just received a second promotion to a more responsible position. He felt that he wouldn't have survived without stress help, and that stress management was providing a vital supportive skill, as well as providing the confidence of being able to come out on top and enjoy his increasing work challenges. Andrew will become a top executive with the necessary survival skills, as well as having first hand understanding of the need for the right training support *before* promotion.

Stress prevention *should* be a management concern, so that they prevent, rather than create stress producing situations. There are other times when work-related stress is self-inflicted.

Wrong Job, Wrong Person

Gary was such a sufferer, but he is improving. Bill was, and most likely still is, because he wouldn't make any positive moves to help himself.

Gary was referred by his doctor after a long history of drugs for this and that anxiety state and nervy twinges. It wasn't until he found himself unable to face the day without a pill that he sought psychological help.

Gary, a sensitive and caring person, had followed his father's advice (strongly given!) to take an accounting degree rather than travel overseas in his youth. Now in his early forties he bitterly regretted following that advice, found it difficult to get over resentment of his father, hated his present job, suffered the hassles of cross-city travelling in twice daily bouts of mounting tension, couldn't cope with his teenagers or his mother-in-law. You name it,

Gary couldn't cope with it. The final straw was to be caught in the midst of a strike. Alas for him, neither one of the strikers, nor a disapproving top executive, but right in the hot seat of the middle management position of having to placate angry customers, report to anxious top management and liase with the strikers.

Gary has always been tense and easily upset, gentle and unassertive. His support strength was a close relationship with a caring wife, but he felt that his current dis-ease was for him to sort out, not for her to bear. This was one of those occasions when everything so long repressed, spilled out at the first interview. None of the seeming irritations were the major contributors to his frustration and long tension history. No, Gary had all his life wanted to be closely involved with his church and dreamt of working in the ministry rather than in accounting. Now, in the throes of mid-life reappraisal he realised that it was now or never. Why did he not apply? His wife didn't want him to? No, it was fear of being rejected. Such a fear can hold so many people back and results in a very long list of suffered stress symptoms indeed. Relieved of the pressures of tension, Gary was able to concentrate on planning for the new directions of his life.

The Entrepreneur Overload

Bill was a fast moving quick breathing restless Type A person who came with the familiar story of — if my doctor hasn't helped me, whatever can you do! As it turned out, nothing. Or at least nothing we've heard about. Bill was the driving, striving, get upwards and onwards entrepreneur who had built his business from nothing to a financially rewarding state which he couldn't relax enough to enjoy. His ulcer never let him. And he could have been helped if he'd got over the block of "I feel such a fool being here, after all business is booming, I must be coping".

He might just as well have said — "I've been successful, how dare you say that I can't cope". But it was his *body* that signalled painfully the not coping. Having to overcome stress is not a sign of weakness. Instead, it is mature sensibility to care for oneself. Top executive ulcers should not be inevitable badges of achievement. They can be avoided. So too can the stress heart attack, if we first take responsibility for our own stress management, and secondly, ensure that our subordinates learn the same techniques, and finally, all work together to build the low stress, high performance work unit.

Who Stresses Whom?

On a pragmatic level, it makes sense for all organisations to have all their personnel taught stress management for stress relief, because freed from tension problems, performance and productivity are the prime concerns.

This is especially important for dealing with the third category of stress problems. Work pressures, time deadlines, and overload were rated by the NZIM groups as the number one contributors to stress problems. The conditions that create these problems are management's concern. As a manager you are failing in the people concern side of your job if you don't make sure that they all know the basic skills of reducing overload pressures —

- time management
- delegating
- organisation — planning
- defining priorities
- goal setting for results

These are all techniques of management which can be learned. So too can the personal skills of stress management. To help you find out just where your stress problems originate, check through the charts in the next chapter, pinpointing any areas of difficulty.

What can you do about a solution?

What do you consider your organisation should do to help the stress problems?

Can you get help for yourself? Or will you continue to suffer?

As a final thought, how do you survive in an organisation for whom everything, but everything, was wanted yesterday? Get out and find a more congenial work climate? Or learn to sift the priorities from the wouldn't-this-be-a-good-idea-to-do, work towards the vital results to the best of your ability, switch off at the end of the day, returning relaxed to enjoy the challenges of the new day. Or get in a stressful frenzy along with everyone else, beginning each day in a muddled state, ending it even more confused and annoyed?

The choice is yours. You decide your comfort zone and keep yourself within. Relax, kill tension, come alive and enjoy work.

Chapter 7

Recognising Reduced Work Fitness

Here are some common stress symptoms which can result from misfit between you and your working environment and dissatisfaction with yourself and your work performance. Do any of these bother you?

Indecision
Increasing number of errors
Feelings of inadequacy
Procrastination
Loss of concentration
Early morning insomnia
Change in habits: workaholic, more time off
Fatigue — always feeling tired
Increased smoking, alcohol, drugs, medication

These are all general symptoms of work ill health — or work ilth if you like. You may have been puzzling over just why you feel apathetic or why you should now need pills to get you through your working day. Now you've discovered that those items listed above that indicate poor performance can indeed be stress symptoms. It's not you that's losing your powers, your skills or your faculties, but there's something bothersome in your environment. Let's investigate further to uncover the culprit.

In this chapter we give several, long, but by no means exhaustive, lists of potential stress producers in the work situation. For each one determine whether it applies to you and then decide your attitude towards each item. Which do you enjoy, and which do you find upsetting. It can be challenging and stimulating to work to deadlines, or it can be a direct route to stress crisis if there's not enough time to unwind, refresh and recharge ready for the next deadline. Commuting time can be a relaxing break between work and family, or it can be a dreaded daily hassle with all the lights at red, the motorway crawling speed only, and the road swarming with mad inconsiderate drivers.

We have within us the power to choose our attitude to everything, even if we don't have the power to change the situation.

After you have checked the list for items which may occur in your working life but do not bother you, and entered in the stress column those things which do annoy, go back to the change column, and decide whether it is the *situation* which can be altered or whether it is your *attitude* that's the biggest contributor to your stress feelings.

We can feel annoyed every morning that we have to fight the traffic or we can play music we enjoy, and take advantage of uninterrupted free-ranging thinking time.

Sometimes we further stress ourselves by perpetuating and extending a hostile climate by passing on the bad feelings given to us. What is your usual response to snappiness from others? If your boss is bad tempered to you, do you pass it on as anger to your subordinate? Can you refuse to take criticism personally or be caught in anger? You'll save yourself a lot of tension if you learn how to respond calmly. You and your attitude contribute to the total picture, so it is important to decide just where the changes toward low-stress working can and should be made — your situation or in yourself?

We believe that each person has an optimal operating level of challenge and tolerance, a balancing between the leisurely niceties of the Country Club atmosphere and the push, push, push for production of the Sweat Shop, that makes for a comfortable working pace and life for them. This "comfort zone" can differ for each person — a challenge to one may be a major obstacle to another, a fast pace to another only medium speed to you, so that it is really up to you to define your own comfort zone. Overall, do you feel that you are working within the tolerance limits of your *"comfort zone"*?

We have divided the check lists into different areas to help you pinpoint the *"discomfort zones"* of your working life. Remember, that it is usual for there to be ups and downs from too little to too much, but if you feel that you are far too often strained to the limits, go through the items and decide what you can change in the situation, and what you can do to change your attitude to a positive outlook.

What things are left that you cannot control and which the organisation must change?

What will you do to survive a hostile work climate — stay or move?

Work Stress Checklist

Job Content	Occurs	Stresses	Suggested Change
Workload: too heavy			
not enough to satisfy			
Time pressures, and deadlines			
Output pressures from other departments			
Working conditions, hours, commuting time			
Taking work home — the bulging briefcase syndrone			
Too much travel away from home			
Other			
Organisation Structure and Policies			
Unclear, or lacking, standards for promotion			
Blocks to promotion — no future			
Poorly defined organisational goals and objectives			
the general "political" climate — competitive or co-operative, apathetic or go ahead			
Uncertainty about organisation or industry future			
Takeover, merger or company re-organisation			
Other			

Work Stress Checklist

Role Related Problems	Occurs	Stresses	Change Needed
Uncertainty about what's expected of you on the job.			
Lack of authority to make decisions related to your job.			
Get the blame for other people's mistakes.			
Information about actual job poor, or no job description.			
Poorly defined responsibiities and range of authority.			
Other			
Relationships with Others			
Prior history of conflict in group, or between certain people.			
Hostility, resentment, no co-operation between departments.			
One particular person always causes you bother, no matter what.			
Threatening or hostile pressure from your boss.			
Unsatisfactory working relationship with your subordinate, your co-workers.			
Other			

Job Quality Pressures

	Occurs	Stresses	Change
Constant requirement of maintaining performance standards.			
Continual effort to keep to high standards.			
Standards — set by quality control or — personal standards for achievement.			
Lack of feedback about performance.			
Some feedback but little constructive criticism.			
Replacement threat from the competition of younger better educated work people.			
Anxiety about job security.			
Fear of failing specific assignments.			
Other			

Here is a simple way to determine if your organisation is most likely to be a high performance — low stress work place. Read through these descriptions of climate and related stress problems to find out which one your organisation most closely resembles.

Country Club

A work climate that is:
overstaffed
few goals
few directives
pleasant
undemanding
nice for everyone

Produces attitudes of:
boredom
restlessness
low output
loss of high achievers

Balanced: High Performance — Low Stress

Challenging Climate:
sufficient staff
clearly defined jobs
specific goals and time framework
worthwhile work
committed workers — creative, enthusiastic, productive.

Sweat shop

A work climate that is:
understaffed —
muddling along
everyone pitching in

Leads to:
undirected effort
restricted output
working to rule
absenteeism

Where do you put your organisation?

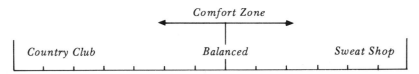

If you have placed it outside the balanced middle, what can be done to reduce stress in the working environment?

Where is your comfort zone? What direction will the move be towards balance? What needs to be changed to bring about balance?

Stress in the Executive Suite

The executive ulcer, seemingly regarded as the evidence of achievement, should be seen clearly for what it is — a result of careless and deliberate misuse of human material. Widespread though the ulcer suffering has been, it's place had been taken by the No. 1 stress killer — coronary heart disease. It's easy to see how the pattern of executive ill-health arises.

He is sedentary rather than active; overindulges on expense account food and wine, travels a lot, suffers jet lag, juggles family and work demands, plays the power game, emerges into the loneliness of the top.

He is frequently overweight, puffs and blows if he ever has to use a flight of stairs instead of the lift, and grows evermore work encrusted as his recreation shrinks to nothing.

She has hitherto escaped this pattern. Women have lived longer, been less prone to the ravages of the stress diseases, ulcers, hypertension, and fewer, far fewer have entered the coronary care stakes.

Alas, the pattern is changing. As women emerge into the management scene, they too are falling victims to the stress syndrome.

The Extra Pressures on Women Executives

In a study of 125 British women executives, fewer physical stress related symptoms were reported than were psychological symptoms of stress, with the exception of migraine headaches, as this table shows.

Women Managers Reporting Physical and Psychological Illness

Physical	%	Psychological	%
Gastric and/or peptic ulcer	4.4	Anger	35.6
Asthma	2.2	Irritation	60.0
High blood pressure	9.6	Anxiety	50.4
Migraine	27.4	Tiredness	69.6
Eczema	5.9	Low self-esteem	25.9
Heart disease	0.0	Depression	23.7
Arthritis and/or rheumatoid arthritis	8.1	Tension (neck or back)	42.2
		Sleeplessness	34.1
Stroke	0.0	Frustration	34.8
		Dissatisfaction with life or job	34.1

(from Personnel Management, June 1980, p.51)

As well as the usual pressures of work, women in senior management positions too often find that they are subject to stresses and strains which bypass their male counterparts with the same organisational status.

These women have commented upon having to cope with:

feelings of isolation as innovators.
prejudice from stereotyping discrimination from colleagues, superiors, subordinates.
promotional blocks within the organisational structure and climate.
conflicting demands between career and marriage/family life.
unrealistic expectations of them as "token women".
achievement pressures: too high, and she's a slavedriver, or too low ... what else would you expect of a woman.

Feelings of isolation, tokenism, and stereotyping limitations can be eased through building a supportive network amongst other women executives across a range of occupations. Quite often you'll find that something you felt was slighting "because you are a woman" is an attitude that's peculiar to that particular industry, or organisation, rather than specific to your department. In other instances, you may find that when other women have had similar experiences, then they also have solutions to share.

Remember to analyse the stress symptom with the two key questions — is environment or attitude to blame? If it is situational — what can be done to correct it, by yourself, by others? If attitude, then what must you do, or alter, not to stress yourself?

At the Top and Later On

As well as the previously listed possible stress producers at work, there are others peculiar to people who reach exalted positions.

Too often they have delusions of being both indispensable and indestructable, as either the Kingpin or the Queen Bee. The result is a refusal to delegate, to share either the power, the glory, or the workload. A confident person builds a supportive group of equal ability people, all contributing to a high performance, less stress climate. The unsure person ensures that self confidence is maintained by lower ability personnel in the work group, withholding recognition for any efforts above this level, discouraging innovation and new ideas which may threaten replacement. The climate is likely to be low performance and high stress for everyone, despite that some persons in the group are willing to give far more in output.

It is painful to acknowledge, even to oneself, that coping difficulties are because of personal limitations. But if you don't you can't possibly acquire the skills — be it people, technical or financial — that will help you.

Superannation, that easement of later life, can be a potent stress factor to the younger person locked into a hated job because moving out will mean loss of money. With family commitments, and mortgage payments, those superannuation contributions cannot afford to be lost by the person who has agonized through a mid-life appraisal and realizes that it is to be now or never if the world is to be dazzled by such artistic endeavours as never seen before. That money would help the restart, the new direction. Without it, the move is never made, and a few years later there's another executive taken from the prime of life by a coronary. A welcome release for the artist forever suppressed by the accountant?

Don't let it happen to you.

Chapter 8

Quality of Life

Relaxation and stress management techniques work towards achieving wellness in every aspect of living, so that you have the skills to put together a life style that is well balanced for you. Contained with the wellness ideal, is the effective person concept. By that we mean confident and competent to cope with any situation or with any person that has the potential to be a stress producer if you allow it to do so.

In mastering the skills needed to put you in control of defining your own individual comfort zone, you've also gained the additional benefits of bringing both your physical and mental health to a peak level. By following the ideas outlined, you will have fulfilled the World Health Organisation's definition of health as a state of full physical, mental and social wellbeing.

The fit person is healthy in the fullest sense with a well balanced life style that is free from dis-ease. It is not enough just to live and work feeling below par, that's just existing. Instead, we believe that the emphasis is on improving the quality of life. By now you should be feeling the benefits in both the work and recreational aspects of your life. We believe that life should be enjoyed. Whatever is the purpose of miserably going on from day to day? Yet far too many people do just that, because they won't begin to apply the simplest of self awareness exercises.

The Stress Management Key

Stress is a misfit between you and your environment. The key to either eliminating the stress producers, or reducing them to manageable proportions is to —

1. *Identify the presence of strain.*
    It's not a weakness to admit to stress, nor should not coping be a matter of shame. Unfortunately, this too often is the case, but you must at the least, admit it to yourself.

2. *Define exactly how you are suffering stress.*
    Is it a physical reaction? Heart attack, indigestion etc? Or

metabolic — weight gain or loss? Or psychological — friction with others? Or are the physical and psychological intertwined — tension headaches?

3. *Locate the stress producers.*
Go through your check lists until you've uncovered a likely culprit. Did you find an overall lack of fitness or recreational allowances? Or identify specific stress situations?

4. *Take the appropriate remedial action.*
After deciding how and what stresses you, counter attack with relaxation techniques for immediate relief, and a plan for long term control. Remember, you need both together to revitalise your body and calm your mind.

Release Your Creative Potential

Relaxed and healthy we come alive to enjoy our life to the full, to extend our potentialities in ever widening circles of achievement in whatever way we decide. Note that this doesn't mean greatness or fame, or financial or occupational success, unless that is our choice. No, it means to stretch a little further, grow a little more, in the directions we feel impelled to make our own.

It may be that freed from the tension of a boring or a too demanding job, of being in the wrong area, that your come alive choice is a new direction, a new job, a changed life style — the one you've always dreamt would be yours. It may be that with relationship tensions minimised, or past responsibilities lessened, you come alive as your own person, enjoying those close to you, while increasing in confidence in doing the things important to you. It may be that realisation that your stress feelings have been self-induced will bring such a change of attitude that you have truly returned to life enjoyment, with your nervous fears, your what-if worry, and negative thinking banished for ever.

Or perhaps the time you've spent in the self-awareness exercises has helped you to pinpoint the situational stress producers, so that with them eliminated, you and your environment are now coexisting in harmonious fitness. Where ever, or however, *you* have made the changes and *you* have the skills to be sure that you never *allow* yourself to be the victim of stress suffering again.

Of course, there will always be some annoyances and difficulties, some problem situations in your future. What a dull life if it were never ruffled! But you won't let difficulties get on top of you.

Instead, take them for the challenges they are and overcome the obstacles with positive thinking and positive plans of counter attack. You'll find that this way, your solutions will be more creative and out of adversity you will find new hope and new directions.

It is an age old truism that adversity strengthens character. Indeed it does, but it's not until it's all over that we can appreciate to the full the strength of our coping or the resources within ourselves, that we hardly knew we possessed. Oh, yes, difficulties can bring out the best in us, but it's so unpleasant while our character is being thus shaped. With the attitude of a saint and the patience of an angel, no doubt we'd not notice the pain. Failing both those attributes, the art of coping through relaxation makes the process at least retrospectively worthwhile.

The Power of Choice

We can of course choose angelic acquiesence, defeatist disengagement, or stress management coping. This power of choosing our attitude is one of the most powerful self help attributes we have. At each apparent blow we have the choice of doing nothing in passive acceptance, or of reacting positively in activities to circumvent circumstances.

The ultimate responsibility for their health and well being rests with each individual person. Here too we can put our choice power to work for us. As well as living from a positive stance, we have the choice to maintain our physical wellbeing through suitable diet, and adequate physical activity, recreation and sleep. Or we can choose to eat too much, drink too much, play to exhaustion, work to burnout and generally treat our bodies as not worth our respect.

What is your choice? Self-inflicted abuse of your body? Or self-cherishing of the outer part of the uniqueness that is you?

Do you take better care of your car than yourself? Some exhausted stress tortured executives have beautiful cars which appear to have never lacked for an oil change or greaseup or attention to squeaks. Alas the driver hasn't time for regular relaxation, let alone for the practising required in learning, wants quick acting, no fuss remedies when little short of a complete overhaul would restore wellbeing.

Why Be Alive
There's one other aspect that we believe important to total wellbeing and that is the finding of a purpose or meaning in our lives.

Self-awareness has been to the fore throughout this book. You first have to know what's really the root source of your stress misfit before you can correct it. You need to know yourself, your abilities, your strengths, your support as well as your responsibilities, if you are to be sure that you're not suffering by being in the wrong place for you.

Do you have answers for:

Where am I going?
Where am I now?
Where do I go from here?

We believe that there has to be challenges, goals, an overall meaning and purpose in life to make it worthwhile to live each day to the full.

Our personal meaning is a blend of many things — time with our families and friends, solitude by the sea or in the bush, sporting activities, music, challenges of potential building in our work, a course of study completed, and so on. The list is endless. There is always a new adventure or a new experience to savour. Tension free you can enjoy it all.

We'd like to leave you with the belief that you too can choose the meaning in your life in the two fold blending of what we *give* to life, our creativity and through what we *take* from life, in many and varied experiences.

Victor Frankl an Austrian born psychiatrist, who put forward the creativity-experience combination, says that the human beings' drive to find meaning goes beyond mere self-expression. Here he brings in his third dimension in the meaning triangle — the freedom to make our own choice about conditions or situations.

He puts it like this, believing that we move between the poles of success and failure.

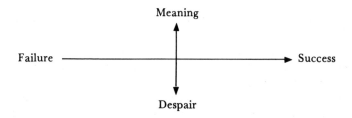

(*Psychotherapy and existentialism*, Frankl. p. 36, Pelican edition)

We believe that the growth path cuts diagonally, like the figure below as one moves from the misery of failure to the success of purpose in life.

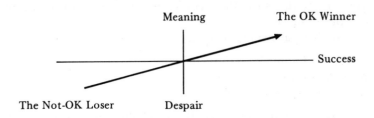

People who come to us for counselling help sometimes feel as though they have fallen to the bottom of the loser line — if you do have such a tendency to let things get on top of you, then take heart that this is a temporary stress result, and you can return to the feelings of confidence and hope as an *OK Winner*.

So much of the difficult to define dissatisfaction of nebulous fears is the search for meaning. The "existential vacuum" Frankl names it of the person who has all the outward signs of having everything but who nevertheless asks "what am I doing here?" and decides that the answer is "nothing worthwhile".

The depressed, the nervy, the tense poor-me person, is focussed too much on the miseries of the situation. Look outward and upward away from yourself, be involved outside of yourself, and your come alive attitude will spark positive strokes from others. You may feel that a search for meaning is too philosophical, too abstract a concept for you. Well, how about a purpose for getting up and going each day. Do you feel that you have that? Or do you feel instead in a dead end and that there is little use in trying to get out of the rut? The key to feeling better is within yourself, but you must be the one to turn it outwards.

Focus outwards to something you enjoy and give always to the best of your ability.

The psychologist Abraham Maslow puts it this way. "If you deliberately plan to be less than you are capable of being, then I warn you that you'll be deeply unhappy for the rest of your life. You will be evading your own capacities, your own possibilities." (From *The Farther Reaches of Human Nature*, p 37, 1973 Pelican edition.) He goes on to say that too often we are afraid of the possibilities that we glimpse within ourselves in our most perfect moments. Then we shiver with awe and fear before these very possibilities.

Surely the meaning and purpose in our lives lies with the challenge of making that promise of our peak potential become the reality of all our dormant talents fulfilled. That's life explored fully, outgoings experienced deeply, and shared with all the joyousness of the person in control of their environment, and at peace with themselves.

You too can take up the challenge of living to release your potential greatness. Free yourself from energy draining tension, relax and come alive.

Chapter 9

Case Studies

Case One: Diane was a married woman in her thirties, with two children of nine and eleven. She was very tense and 'nervy' and was showing symptoms of stress. She slept badly, was irritable with her husband and children, cried for the least little thing and couldn't stand noise. Even the normal noise of her children playing was enough to make her scream at them to be quiet. Her husband had been sympathetic to her complaints at first, but as the years went by he became more and more fed up and had reached the stage where he labelled her 'neurotic'.

Diane had consulted her family doctor about her condition, two years previously, and had asked him for some tranquillisers. She had been seen for a quick five minutes, told there was nothing wrong with her, and to pull herself together, refused tranquillisers, and ushered out the door. Her doctor was an elderly man who did not believe in 'all that nonsense'. The advice he gave her was to keep busy and involved and in time all would come right. After that experience Diane refused to see another doctor, though her husband tried to get her to do so.

The reason Diane eventually decided to seek the help of a psychological clinic was because she discovered that her husband was having an affair with another woman, and she was frightened of losing him altogether. As she said herself "The way I am what man would want to live with me anyway."

Diane was not a good subject for relaxation at first; she fought it all the way. She didn't like the voice on the tape, found the message boring, didn't have the time to do it anyway, couldn't see that it could possibly achieve anything etc. She put up so many objections that in the end we asked her whether or not she really wanted to help herself. This made Diane think, and she began to realise that she had been looking for somebody to wave a magic wand and solve all her problems. When she came to the conclusion that the only person who could help her was herself, and that we could only offer guidance and support she decided to start working for herself. She underwent a course of counselling and at the same time continued with her relaxation programme . . . this time with a positive attitude.

Within one month Diane was feeling less tense and was sleeping better. She experienced a tingling sensation in her legs when she relaxed, but when it was explained to her that this was nothing to worry about, she ceased to be concerned about it. Three weeks later the tingling went and did not return. By this stage Diane was starting to feel a lot better in herself. She was able to tolerate the children's noise better, and was not so irritable with them. She also started to feel that she could cope better with the daily situations that arose in her life.

Her husband, seeing the change in her, started to once more become interested in her, and eventually resumed sexual relations with her. He told her that he now felt new hope for their marriage. To date Diane is continuing with her relaxation programme, though counselling has stopped, and is continuing to improve.

Case Two: Don was a good worker, so good that his firm promoted him to foreman. The trouble was that when Don received his promotion he started to worry about every aspect of his new job. He has always been known as 'a bit of a perfectionist' but now his compulsion to do everything perfectly assumed enormous proportions. He began to check and double check everything, to 'nitpick' both at work and home, and to be totally unable to get away from his work. He took it home with him, and even thought about it when he was in bed at night.

Don was in the obsessive behaviour syndrome, and was functioning within a very rigid framework. If anything unusual happened, or things happened out of the normal order, he would be completely thrown and almost go to pieces. He was rigid and inflexible in the extreme.

When it became obvious, even to Don, that he was heading for a collapse, he decided to seek help. At first he said that he had only come to see if the quality of his sleep could be improved because he was unable to let go of work worries after he had gone to bed at night.

Gradually as he felt more at ease with counselling the whole story started to emerge. It seems that Don had been continually put down by his parents when he was a child. His father had had an unrealistically high expectation of him (which he could never reach) and had frequently told him he would never make it in life. That he was hopeless, useless etc. Because of this Don had developed a low self esteem, and was constantly trying to prove himself to himself. Hence the perfectionist obsession. In his own eyes he never did things well enough, never really completed anything, and could certainly never reach his own impossibly high standards.

Don fortunately responded well to relaxation therapy, and within a few weeks was showing marked improvement. He also entered into a programme of stress management, which helped him cope with his work, and explored through counselling the factors in his early childhood and present attitude towards himself, that were causing him to act in the way he was.

He found the time-slot relaxation exercise an invaluable aid in reducing tension before it reached a high level, and frequently applied this throughout the day. He didn't wait for regular times but used it whenever he felt tension building up.

Around the two month mark Don reported that he was experiencing a marked reduction in tension, and was coping with the stress of his job much better. He was sleeping better at night and was no longer taking his work home with him.

Shortly after that Don became very busy at work and neglected to do his regular daily relaxation exercise. The pressure was on to such an extent that he also forgot about his time-slot exercise. Within two weeks the old symptoms were reappearing, though in a much milder form. Nevertheless their reappearance was enough to convince Don that no matter how busy he got he could not afford to forget to relax and break tension daily. The principle of 'the busier you are the more you need to make time for relaxation' was brought home to him very clearly through this situation.

Don is now making steady progress and is managing his home and work life in a much better way. He is no longer coming for treatment but is making sure that he keeps up with his relaxation every day, and continues putting into effect the guidelines he has been given.

Case Three: Leon's problem was knots in the stomach. He said he had a continual sensation of tension in the stomach area, and this was with him day and night. Sometimes it lessened, but it never entirely left him. He had believed that there was something physically wrong with him that was causing this problem, and accordingly had sought medical help. When all the tests proved that he was physically alright his doctor suggested that tension might be the cause of his problem, and suggested he consult us. Acting on this advice he came along to see what we could do to help.

We had some difficulty in convincing Leon that tension could actually cause the physical discomfort he was experiencing. His reasoning was, I am experiencing a physical sensation, there must be a physical reason. He couldn't see how just relaxing for a period of time every day could get rid of the knots in his stomach. When he finally grasped the principle of relaxation he agreed to give it a try, though he still had some difficulty in translating knots in the stomach to tension.

In view of his scepticism Leon made good progress. He reported feeling physically better within two weeks, though the stomach tension had only lessened slightly. A week and a half later he said that his concentration had improved to a marked degree. It was at this stage that Leon accepted that relaxation therapy was actually doing something for him, and that it could work.

Leon at this time began to realise that he had another problem which was adding to his tension. He could not express his feelings. He had never been able to do so, and all his life he had disowned and negated them. As with a lot of boys he had been conditioned to believe that to have feelings and especially to express them was 'sissy' so consequently he had always suppressed them. He came from a family that showed little or no emotion, and this had added to his problem. He stated that he could never once remember being kissed or cuddled as a child by his father, and that his mother used to kiss him 'on special occasions' such as his birthday. With a background like this it would be surprising if he did know how to express normal emotion.

In addition to relaxation therapy Leon received help in learning to own and express his feelings. When he understood what disowning his feelings all those years had done to him he made the comment "I guess my feelings all went to my stomach instead of coming out". He wasn't far out in his assessment.

It took about three months of regular relaxation for Leon to lose the knots in his stomach, but fortunately in the end he did so. Though the stomach area was certainly the last part that responded to relaxation therapy. Even now if he becomes tense or overtired Leon feels his stomach starting to tense up, though he is not aware of tension in any other part of the body. However he knows how to break tension quickly now, and immediately applies his relaxation exercise before it has a chance to build up too much.

Many people have an area of the body that is particularly prone to tension. With some people it is their head, or neck, or back or chest. With Leon it was his stomach. We should be aware of which area of the body is our 'Achilles heel' and during our relaxation times, particularly concentrate on conditioning our trouble-spot to relax.

Case Four: Dorothy had suffered from 'her nerves' as she termed it, for years. She had been to two psychiatrists and had been in hospital twice to try and overcome her feelings of anxiety and depression. Dorothy was deeply steeped in negativism, and was very doubtful that anything could help her. Nevertheless she was willing to try relaxation because she had heard of a couple of people whom it had really helped.

She learned about it and took a relaxation tape home to try out. In addition to this she was given some constructive guidelines to follow to help lift her out of her depression. To each suggestion that was made Dorothy had a "yes but" reply. There were reasons why anything and everything that was suggested would not work for her. It became obvious that she was totally emeshed in a negative spiral.

Though every effort was made to help her Dorothy did not improve. She was convinced in her own mind that nothing could help her, so of course nothing did. She was unwilling to work for herself or make any changes. When she realised that only she could help herself and that she was going to have to work in order to do so, she gave up.

She did not respond to relaxation therapy, and in the end gave it up, saying that she found it tedious to have to practise it daily. Occasionally Dorothy makes an appointment to come into the centre and off-load her problems. All she wants is for somebody to listen to her; she will not explore her options and take notice of any suggestion for improving her situation, that is put to her. It is doubtful that Dorothy can or ever will be helped. She has made up her mind that nothing is ever going to work for her and that is that. Deep seated negativism such as this is self-defeating. Unfortunately Dorothy is, and is likely to remain, one of life's casualties.

Case Five: Julie didn't have any very serious problems, but she had been feeling vaguely depressed for a long time. She was prone to headaches, and tended to over-react to situations at times. She often felt that she was more tense than she should be, and at these times described herself as feeling 'woolly-headed'. Julie decided to do something to help herself after a chat with her doctor, who told her that there was no need for her to continue putting up with these symptoms.

She began a course of relaxation, and almost immediately started to respond. The first thing she noticed was that she didn't have a headache for a month . . . previously she had averaged three a month. She mentioned that when she did her relaxation she often experienced a desire to cry. She was encouraged to do so, and told that this was a healing thing . . . it was simply the mind trying to off-load its deep seated tension and frustrations. Suppressed emotions were also being given a chance to surface. When Julie understood this, she let the tears flow when she felt the urge to. Within six weeks she no longer felt the desire to cry during relaxation, and was feeling considerably better in other areas as well. Her feelings of depression abated, and she felt more self-motivated than she had for a long time.

Julie continued to respond well to relaxation; she felt so much better in most ways that she determined to keep it up even when she no longer felt the need of it. She stated that she had not enjoyed life so much for years. Within three months Julie had grasped relaxation so well that she no longer needed to use the tape on a regular basis. She only used it when she felt she wasn't 'letting go' sufficiently on her own, when applying her daily relaxation exercises. Julie has now convinced her family of the benefits of relaxation, and they have all joined her in doing it.

Case Six: Stuart came to us because he was experiencing feelings of panic when called upon to tackle anything that demanded mental effort. His mind would 'go blank' at these times, and he would feel unable to cope. In addition to this he was suffering from occasional fits of shaking. These would happen at the most unexpected times, in bed at night as well as when he was in situations that caused mild stress. Stuart was the youngest of seven children; from his description of his childhood he had certainly been emotionally deprived. In addition he said that he gave up trying to express his opinion or stand up for his rights at a very early age because he was always 'howled down' by his older brothers and sisters.

As a result he had formed the habit of saying as little as possible, and letting people walk all over him. Stuart had a lot of suppressed anger inside him, some of which dated back for years. He was helped to express this, and shown how to handle his anger and express it. His shaking and inability to cope were the direct result of these problems.

Stuart was slow to respond to relaxation at first, he didn't experience any benefits or notice any change for a month. However during the second month things began to happen. The first thing he noticed was that his fits of shaking became more spaced out and lessened in intensity. He was by this time applying time-slot relaxation as well, and used this to good effect to cope with his rising feelings of panic when confronted with jobs involving mental effort.

Once he realised that relaxation was working for him, and that he could handle his panic and eventually overcome his shaking fits, Stuart went from strength to strength. He became far more confident in his handling of situations. He learned to relax immediately if he felt he was becoming tense; he also learned to speak up for himself more, and this made him feel less tense because he was no longer bottling up thoughts and feelings to the same extent.

During the third month Stuart only experienced shaking fits on two occasions, which was exceptionally good considering that he had a broken engagement during this time. He also reached the decision that he was going to take a course in self-assertion because to quote him "People have been pushing me around all my life, and now I've discovered that I don't have to let them do it". Taking this course raised his self esteem and made him feel still more confident. After the third month all fits of shaking stopped, and have not returned for a considerable time now. Stuart very occasionally experiences some of the old panic feelings when he is under stress, but knows how to deal with them, and does so quickly and effectively.

Case Seven: Shelley, at 14 years old, was one of our youngest clients.

She was already a chronic worrier who would destroy herself and the career she aspired to if she did not learn how to deal with stress soon. Fourteen years is far too young to be under treatment for an ulcer.

Shelley wanted to be a ballet dancer and her whole life was ballet-practice, examinations, recitals, and always more and more practise. She was good, and it did indeed seem very likely that she would gain a place to a prestigious ballet company.

To be sure that she gave herself every possible chance she practised and practised and practised, forever correcting mistakes, concentrating on technique, never completely satisfied with the turn of the ankle here or the pointing of the toe there. Shelley was a perfectionist who set herself impossibly high standards. To fall below, to lose competition points, was a disaster she couldn't cope with. She blamed herself for not doing better and she drove herself into more and yet more time practising.

She neglected her school work — other subjects were such a bore. They weren't dancing! And if all this wasn't enough, she worried constantly about dying.

Shelley was referred by her doctor, in response to her very anxious mother's request for help. Her mother could see her daughter going from day to day into an ever more stressful state, but just didn't know where to start in giving help.

We began with the basic relaxation training to reduce the body tension to help that ulcer heal. The next stage was a desensitization programme to get examination and public performance fears under control. For a young lady who aimed for a life of first nights, that was vital to her future wellbeing. The final step in the teaching was for Shelley to understand how to apply stress management techniques to her particular situation.

Although we had dealt with the fear of performing as a *fear*, we also had to work for the control of pre-performance tension. If she didn't master that, then there was little hope that either her mental or her physical health would be enough for the demanding career she had chosen. Shelley was an enthusiastic relaxation learner, for she would try anything to help her come out top, so it wasn't long before she could apply time-slot relaxation before performances.

It was then that she noticed for herself the benefits we'd expected her to gain. The quality of her dancing improved, yet she wasn't striving anywhere near as hard as previously. Her body, freed from the tension of striving, responded even more creatively. It was as though all that effort which had gone into worrying was now re-channelled into performance effort.

There remained but one issue to discuss with Shelley and this one she wasn't quite ready to accept. This was the idea of balance to her life. Right now dancing was overshadowing everything else, but it was important that she reached an adequate school standard to ensure her acceptance at ballet school. She understood that. What we did want her to understand, was that if she denied herself the many experiences of a world outside of dancing, that her dancing would begin to reflect this. There would be nothing to draw on to put meaning and creativity into her work.

Her dancing would become stale through not using recreational time to refresh her spirit as well as her body. In time, we feel that she will realize this and develop interests outside of her dancing.

Now that she has learned that the coping skills vital to surviving in a demanding career also enhance the technical skills of her dancing, Shelley has a far greater hope of being a prima ballerina.

Case Eight: Steve came in with so many stress difficulties that he really thought he was in such a hopeless mess that help was almost impossible.

Steve had completed his law degree a year previously and was very pleased when he was accepted into a reputable firm. The pleasure of the appointment had long since been replaced by the pain and pressures of a demanding practice. Now he reported sweating attacks, hands that trembled around the office coffee cups and the horrors of sleepless nights when every aspect of the day's court activities whirled around and around in his mind. It was impossible to switch off and sleep as he reviewed the stresses of his working day.

Unrefreshed, he'd wake in the early hours, dreading the events and people who'd crowd into the coming day's schedule, each bringing problems he'd have to solve, or fight.

Fighting was what Steve's life was all about now — fighting everyone elses battle, fighting for survival, fighting his body strain to keep going. If life was such an effort to keep going at 21, would he ever survive to see forty?

Steve suffered agonisingly for a year before seeking help. Three weeks after his first visit, he was beginning to find life bearable again — he could relax enough to get a good night's sleep. For the person tortured by stress to breaking point, this first sleep without a mind in turmoil is like a miracle. It's just so sad that they wait so long for the sinple healing of relaxation, because they don't know where to go for help.

The next step in Steve's healing was the report that he could face a working day without trembling.

At about this time, we were into the life style analysis part of the programme, pinpointing the problems in the work situation.

Steve was experiencing that oh, so common transition from student to a practitioner of all the skills of training and education.

It takes time to be comfortable in a first working environment, and it takes time to find out which skills move easily from textbook to consumer use, and which ones need adjustment here and there in their practical application. Steve had gotten through this phase he though quite well, when suddenly it happened.

His ability earned him the court work, and his stress problems. Steve took on the whole world's problems with each client and each night he replayed the day's actions, complete with the additional highlights of self-criticism — If only I'd done this . . . or done that . . . or said that . . . or summed up brilliantly and logically, devastated the opposition. Hindsight helps us all win the fights, but not at the expense of sleep.

What Steve had to do here was to accept for himself the standard that he had worked to the best of his ability in his client's interests — and switch off from that problem, that client at that point. No rehashing at night time, but if there were points that came back to disappoint him, then decide what would have been a better course of action, and file that away as a learning experience, not a disaster experience.

In this sort of stress problem, where learning this is an important part of skill development and confidence is built through experiences, then it's helpful to keep a notebook handy, write in the difficulty followed by the solution hindsight suggests as more appropriate, and file it all somewhere that only you see.

That way, you relieve your mind of reliving tension, and you have a ready reference of learning anecdotes. The notebook will also come in handy when you're famous and successful and look for inspiration for your lectures, your after dinner speeches and your memoirs.

Steve was a young man tensed from head to toe when he first arrived for counselling. He found the relief from muscular tension unbelievably relaxing. He just didn't realize that his body was so tense. In the exercises of checking out muscle group tension, he became aware of the source of his neck and shoulder pains. Every time a client walked through his office door, Steve leant forward on his desk and braced himself, tensing from the arms up, waiting to be hit by the problems coming his way.

Once Steve became aware of this self-inflicted tension, he taught himself to deliberately relax when his clients approached. You will not be surprised to know that Steve's tension headaches have disappeared.

Self-help Tapes

There are five self-help learning tapes available, for people who wish to acquire further skills. These reinforce the message of Iris Barrow's books. They are:

1 Learning to relax Five, ten-minute mental and physical relaxation exercises. Where two exercises are listened to daily, improvement usually takes place within 3 weeks.

2 Understanding and overcoming stress All about understanding, identifying and learning how to cope with stress. Practical ways of overcoming and controlling it.

3 Understanding and overcoming depression A series of simple steps to help overcome depression and prevent its recurrence. Better ways of functioning outlined.

4 Raising your self esteem Methods for raising self esteem (includes exercises). Having a good self esteem is vital to mental and emotional wellbeing... we can only act 'out there' according to how we feel within ourselves.

5 How to build your confidence Ways of building confidence, based on acting as we wish to become, and feeding in positive messages to achieve results, and help us grow on all levels.

Tapes may be ordered by phone (Auckland 534-2697). Or by posting the order form below to Mrs Carol Cross, C/- 13 Hostel Access Rd, Eastern Beach, Auckland, New Zealand.

Please send me (tick)

1	( )	Learning to relax	$10.50
2	( )	Understanding and overcoming stress	$10.50
3	( )	Understanding and overcoming depression	$10.50
4	( )	Raising your self esteem	$10.50
5	( )	How to build your confidence	$10.50

Price includes full set of instruction sheets, postage and packaging.
Tapes 60 minutes.

One tape	$10.50	Four tapes	$37.50
Two tapes	$19.50	Five tapes	$46.00
Three tapes	$28.50		

N.B. Discount applies to any combination of tapes.

I enclose M/O, P/N, Cheque for ....

Please post tape(s) to   NAME ....

ADDRESS ....

....